Zeus

Best wishes,
Shelagh

Zeus

Shelagh Paton-Ash

For Mark,

and for Pit Bulls everywhere.

Dogs are not our whole life, but they make our lives whole.
-ROGER CARAS

Why does watching a dog be a dog fill one with happiness?
-JONATHAN SAFRAN FOER

Prologue

The cyclist accelerates as he hits the downward slope on Olympic Drive. The cool February air tears at his jersey as he pedals ferociously towards home. It is pure exhilaration; he feels like he is flying.

It's a triathlon bike, built for aerodynamics, and the cyclist's body is crouched, his back almost parallel with the road. His forearms rest on the aerobars, and his hands are thrust far forward and close together, lightly gripping the extended handles.

Coming the other way, on the opposite side of the road, is a large, red pick-up truck. A Ford F-150. The cyclist is unconcerned as he watches the truck slow down. Then, as if from very far away, he perceives that the truck is turning, directly and unhesitatingly across his path, and in a moment of acute clarity he realizes the driver has no idea he is there.

The collision is head-on. Unavoidable. Curiously, the bicycle itself remains on the road, pushed perforce backwards by the still-moving truck — but the cyclist flies, seemingly weightless, over the top of the vehicle, and lands, crumpled, on the edge of the sidewalk.

The driver of the truck throws open his door and runs back towards the inert body, frantically dialing 911. Then he prays.

The cyclist remains motionless on the side of the road as strangers rush in, the horror of the moment reflected in their pale, shocked faces.

All sound is sucked out of the afternoon until, at last, the wail of distant sirens breaks the awful hush, and the bystanders back away, making a respectful space for the blaring vehicles.

One

October 2007

It was a chilly autumn morning in the small university town of Athens, Georgia. A grey pick-up truck swung into the wooded parking lot of the animal shelter and stopped in front of the large, low building. A young man climbed awkwardly out of the truck, slammed the door, and headed towards the entrance. He walked with the rolling gait of someone who has suffered a traumatic injury. His right hip and leg were strong and well-muscled, but his left side was withered and unable to carry its share of weight. He pushed open the door of the pound and limped in.

When he greeted the woman behind the desk, she looked up and smiled. "I'm glad you could come in today, Mark. Just fill out the volunteer sheet and you can go straight back and start walking the dogs."

He wrote his name and time of arrival in the book, then headed towards the area where the dogs were kept. He was greeted by a tremendous chorus of barks, howls and yaps, wagging tails and wet noses pushed up against metal cages. He breathed in the distinctive smell of the pound. A pungent mixture of dog-smells and disinfectant. Not too unpleasant. He walked along next to the cages, greeting each of the dogs.

Some knew him and sniffed his hand eagerly through the bars of their gates. Others stood back, barking nervously; Mark attempted to coax them forward with a few quiet words.

Halfway down the row he came to a cage that was completely quiet. He peered inside and saw, in the far corner, a small Pit Bull, huddled up against the wire. The Pit Bull was the color of toffee, with huge, liquid brown eyes. Mark felt a surge in his chest. He crouched down to talk to the dog, and was rewarded with a hesitant tail wag, but the dog remained where he was, as far from the front of the cage as he could get. The name card on the gate said "Zeus".

He tried calling the dog by his name, but there was no sign of recognition. It must be a name the pound staff had given him.

"I'll be back soon," he said quietly. "I have a few dogs to walk, and then I'll come by and see you again."

As he stood up and continued down the row of cages, he noticed that the dog was keeping his eye on him, even moving a little closer to the front of his cage so as not to lose sight of him. It made him smile.

After walking a few of the other dogs, Mark headed back to the quiet cage and knelt down. The dog had been lying with his head resting on his two front paws, but he sat up as soon as Mark reappeared, and watched him carefully. He had a broad head with roundly-muscled jaws and forehead, and his muzzle was perfectly square in shape. His ears were uneven – one up and one down – and Mark noticed that the tips of both ears were, ever so slightly, quivering.

"Don't be scared," he whispered, "I won't hurt you."

As he chatted quietly, he noticed the dog's ears were moving back and forth. He appeared to be listening to Mark's every word. He had deep frown lines on his forehead, as if he was carrying all the cares of the world on his shoulders.

After a while, the dog stood up and took a few cautious steps towards Mark. He was very thin – his ribs were clearly visible through his coat – but despite that, he had the broad chest, strong shoulders and powerful hind-quarters typical of his breed. He was a very handsome dog.

Mark could see the dog was afraid of him, but there was something in his eyes that gave Mark the impression the dog wanted to trust him. There was a hesitant hopefulness in the way he looked at Mark. Perhaps someone had been kind to him somewhere along the way.

"I'll try taking you for a walk tomorrow, Zeus," he said, "but first I need to find out what your story is."

He eased back up onto his feet and walked his unsteady walk back to the front office, all the way feeling those two brown eyes on his back.

*

Filling out the volunteer sheet at the pound the following day, Mark enquired about the new Pit Bull.

"He was brought in by animal control," said the no-nonsense woman who was manning the front desk. "Had no collar or tag, and he was loitering around a neighborhood where the people weren't too keen on stray Pit Bulls." She shook her head impatiently. "It appears he was mistreated, because he's very scared of humans, particularly men, and he's very malnourished."

"Is he aggressive?" Mark asked.

She looked up at Mark then, smiling brightly. "No, not at all. He allowed us to examine him all over, even inside his mouth. He shook violently the whole time, but he never once showed any signs of aggression. He's just very timid, and dead-scared of people."

"Do you think I could try walking him today?" Mark asked.

"I don't see why not," she said. "See if you can persuade him to go with you."

The knowledge that the little Pit Bull was not aggressive made him happy, and he felt a little spring in his step as he limped towards the cage, quiet amidst the mad cacophony of the pound.

This time, when he stopped in front of the cage, the dog got up immediately and walked with a little more confidence to the gate. As soon as Mark opened the door, though, he backed up into the far corner. Mark could see the whole of his small body trembling, and that his eyes had become huge with fear.

"It's okay, boy," he said gently, lowering himself into a crouching position and turning his body so he wasn't facing him directly. He had learned that approaching a shy dog in this way was far less intimidating. He remained like this for some time, speaking softly. He knew the dog was listening. Then, ever-so-slowly, he lifted his hand and gently stroked one trembling shoulder. He half-expected the dog to move away, but he stayed where he was and allowed Mark to continue stroking him. His coat was soft and smooth, despite his poor condition. As Mark was absently admiring the silky feel of it, he became aware that the dog had stretched out his neck towards him, and was tentatively sniffing him. He felt the warm breath on the side of his neck, and this small gesture from the dog touched him deeply. He kept very still, giving him time to take in his scent. Then he slowly lifted his head, and their eyes met.

Two

Mark made the decision not to walk the dog that day, but rather to take a little more time to gain his trust. He reluctantly left the cage to walk some of the other dogs, who barked with excitement as he approached.

Mark loved dogs, and knew he had a way with them. He had never known life without at least one dog at home, and they had always been important members of the family. He and his siblings had sworn they would never marry someone who wasn't a dog-lover. He wanted to have his own dog, but he was almost finished with his degree, and he was planning to live somewhere else afterwards – possibly California or Colorado – and still deciding whether to look for a job or further his education. Either way, his future was too unclear to consider having a pet. Also, all three of the friends he shared a house with had dogs, so he wasn't short of canine companionship. He would have dogs of his own one day, but now was not the time.

As soon as his classes were over the next day, Mark hurried back to the shelter. He was anxious to see the little Pit Bull. When he reached the dingy pen, he felt a wave of relief that the dog's owners hadn't found him and taken him home. Once again, he crouched down and was rewarded by an immediate response from the dog. This time his tail wagged freely, and his ears were pulled back and low. He dipped his head down as he walked right up to the front of his cage.

Mark felt much more comfortable going into the cage this time. He bent down, touched the dog's broad head, and stroked his bony ribcage down to his tail. Then he gave him a good long scratch behind the ears. The dog stood very still, head hanging down, and when Mark eventually stopped petting him, he looked up gravely from under his eyebrows, the whites of his eyes showing below the dark brown irises.

*

On the fourth day, Mark took a long, appraising look at Zeus and decided it was time to try and get him out of the cage for a walk.

As usual, he stooped down and clambered awkwardly into the cage. Easing himself down onto the floor, he talked calmly to the dog, giving him time to relax. Then, with great gentleness, he eased the leash over Zeus's chunky, square head. There was a clearly defined mark on his neck from years of being tied up, and Mark was afraid the leash would make him shy away. But he seemed comfortable enough, and didn't flinch as it settled around his neck.

Mark began to move slowly towards the gate, tugging gently on the leash and encouraging the dog to follow. Zeus took a couple of hesitant steps, then stopped just outside the threshold of the cage. He stood there, quite still, looking uncertainly around him. Then his tail came out from between his legs and he surged forward, nearly pulling Mark off his feet.

Once Mark had steadied himself, he got a strong grip on the leash and tried to persuade Zeus to walk politely by his side, but the concept completely evaded the Pit Bull, who continued to pull with all his might. It was obvious to Mark that the little fellow had never been walked before. It would take some time and patience to teach him.

The dog was still nervous, and with every bang or strange noise he stiffened and looked around warily. But as the days went by his confidence grew, and it seemed to dawn on him that, maybe, there was no need to pull so hard. The walks gradually became easier and more enjoyable for both of them.

Mark soon found that he couldn't stay away from the dog, and he visited the pound daily – often twice a day, if he had the time. As soon as he arrived he would hurry towards Zeus's cage, trying to suppress the nagging fear that when he got there he would find it empty. He was all too aware that this was a kill-shelter; they were only able to keep unclaimed dogs for a limited time. Almost worse was the possibility that his owners would find him, and take him back to the hell he'd escaped. But every day, as Mark reached the cage, there it was: the face pushed up against the wire, greeting him with unabashed delight.

After an enthusiastic hello, they would head to the outdoor exercise area. Sometimes there were other dogs there, and Mark was happy to see that the Pit Bull showed no aggression towards any of them. On the contrary, he seemed to love their company.

As he became less fearful, Zeus started playing with any dog that was out there, and it became apparent that other dogs liked him. He was submissive, yet friendly, and he soon became a favorite playmate. Mark realized this dog had no idea he was a Pit Bull, and neither did the other dogs. It was only humans who had pre-conceived ideas about different breeds. It was human treatment, too, that shaped the personalities of dogs. This little Pit Bull had no idea that humans bred his type to fight. By nature, he was a friendly, playful dog, without a mean bone in his body. Was that perhaps why he'd been abandoned?

An incident one day, though, made it clear to everyone that not all Pit Bulls were as sweet and harmless as this one. Mark had just put the leash on Zeus and was leading him towards the exercise area, when one of the other volunteers shouted a warning. He looked up. A massive Pit Bull was running towards them across the yard. The dog's eyes were locked on Zeus's small figure, and there was no mistaking his intentions. Time seemed to slow down as Mark registered what was happening. He glanced down at the vulnerable little creature next to him – noticed the sudden stillness of his body, the slight trembling of the uneven ears – and he knew without doubt what was about to happen. His response was unthinking: pure instinct. He bent down, grabbed Zeus, and lifted him high above his head. Luckily, the bigger dog had no interest in attacking humans. His target was the small Pit Bull, which was now up in the air, out of his reach. He jerked to a stop at Mark's feet and glared up at Zeus. Then he lunged over and over again towards the dangling paws, to no avail, each time landing heavily back on all fours.

It seemed like ages that Mark stood there holding Zeus above his head, though in reality it was probably just a few seconds before help arrived and the attacker was hauled away. He lowered the dog to the floor, then, and knelt down next to him. As they looked shakily into each other's eyes, Mark could have sworn that the dog understood what had just happened.

*

On a sunny afternoon two weeks later, Mark arrived at the pound and greeted the staff as usual. He was about to head through to Zeus's cage when one of them called him over. He immediately knew something was wrong.

"Mark," said the staff member, his eyes sliding away towards the floor, "you know that little Pit Bull you like so much?"

"Zeus?" Mark asked nervously.

"Yeah, that's the one. I'm sorry to tell you this, because we've all noticed what a strong bond you've formed with him, but we're going to have to put him to sleep tomorrow."

Mark felt the blood rush to his face, and his heart began thumping in his chest.

"Why? Why would you put him to sleep? There's nothing wrong with him, is there?"

"No, there's nothing wrong with him. It's just that we're only allowed to keep Pit Bulls for two weeks. If they're not claimed or adopted by then, we have to euthanize them. It's the policy here. In fact we've already kept him way longer than we should because we like him. He really seems to be a nice dog, but we can't put it off any longer."

A mixture of frustration and panic welled up in Mark's stomach, and lodged in his throat as a huge, painful lump. He couldn't allow this to happen.

"What can I do?" he almost shouted. "How can I keep him from being put down?"

"Well there are two options," he was told. "You can either adopt him, or you can foster him."

"That's it? Either I take him, or he dies?"

"Yes," the man said quietly, "I'm sorry. We have no choice."

Zeus knew the uneven sound of Mark's footsteps, and no matter what time of day Mark came, he was always there, already waiting for him, mouth wide open and tail wagging vigorously. Mark knelt down and put his arms around the muscular little neck. He was embarrassed to feel tears welling up. He stroked the dog gently, and looked into his eyes.

"I promise I won't let anything bad happen to you," he whispered fiercely. "I'll figure something out and you'll be fine."

The dog looked up at him with wise old eyes, then he shifted his weight and leaned heavily against Mark. The warmth of the dog's body was comforting, and he wrapped his arms around him again and breathed in his pleasant, doggy smell. As he held him close, he thought back to the day when Zeus had been charged by the other Pit Bull. Mark had known then, from the way Zeus had stood there with no intention of fighting back, that there wasn't an ounce of aggression in him. And he knew now, with complete certainty, that he would find a way to keep this dog. It felt right, the two of them together.

Three

November 2007

It was already quite late at night in South Africa when my cell phone rang on the bedside table. My husband and I were staying in my childhood home for the last time; we'd flown to Johannesburg in order to help my elderly parents move from their home of forty-four years into a retirement village. I sat up and reached hurriedly for the phone, afraid it might wake them.

"Hi Mom. It's Mark."

His voice sounded flat, and I immediately knew something was wrong. Since his accident, I was primed for bad news, especially when calls came at this late hour.

"Hi darling," I said, worried, "what is it?"

"Mom, you know how I'm volunteering at the pound?" He paused briefly, then rushed on. "There's this dog there that I really love, Mom, and they're planning to put him to sleep tomorrow!"

"I see," I said cautiously. I could hear his agitation now, but all I was feeling was relief. My husband, Rory, had already picked up on the anxiety in my voice, and he sat bolt upright next to me with a worried frown. I signaled to him that everything was okay, and watched him lie down again. Then I turned my attention back to the phone.

"Why are they putting him to sleep?" I asked.

"Because he's a Pit Bull, and if they're not claimed or adopted in two weeks they just put them down!"

I paused, trying to think of the right thing to say.

It didn't help. "A Pit Bull!" I blurted. "Really?"

"You'd have to meet him, Mom. He's the sweetest dog. I can't let them do that to him!"

I closed my eyes and took a deep breath. "What can you do to save him?"

"I can either adopt him, or foster him."

"Really?" I asked suspiciously. "There's no other way?"

"That's what they told me. If I don't take him, they'll put him down tomorrow."

There was a long silence. I didn't want to say the wrong thing again. Mark knew I wasn't keen on him getting a dog – I strongly disapproved of people who went to work and left their dogs home alone all day. My position was that people shouldn't own dogs if they couldn't take good care of them. But I was a dog-lover too, and I wasn't about to let a dog be put to death if I could help it.

"Listen," I said at last, "you go ahead and foster him, and when Dad and I get back from our trip, we'll help you find a home for him."

"Thanks, Mom," Mark sighed, and I could almost hear the tension leaving his body. I was pretty sure he was planning to save the dog with or without my blessing, but I could tell he was happy to have me on his side. Plus, he knew I could persuade his dad to go along with the plan.

Four

November 2007

Zeus had been granted a stay of execution. But before he could start his new life, he had to spend a little time at the veterinary clinic: not only did he have to get all his vaccinations, but he also had to be neutered and micro-chipped.

Mark was told that he could pick him up three days later, when all his papers would be ready for signing. It was disappointing to have to wait, but it would give him time to get to the pet shop and buy essentials like food, bowls, and a collar and leash. He was very excited about adopting Zeus, and wanted help choosing just the right things for the dog. He knew someone else who would be as excited as he was.

His younger sister was a sophomore at the University of Georgia, and she lived quite close by, in her sorority house. He dialed her number.

"Andrea, are you busy on Friday afternoon?" he asked, trying to sound casual.

"I don't think so. Why?"

"I was wondering if you could come with me to pick up my dog from the vet," he said nonchalantly.

Her reaction was just what he'd hoped for. Of *course* she would come with him on Friday. "Does Mom know?" she asked.

"Yes, but she thinks I'm just going to keep him 'till we can find him a home."

"And you're not planning to do that?"

"I'll never give him up. You'll see why when you meet him."

*

They could hardly wait to get to the pet shop after Friday's classes. They huddled together over the rack with the collars, deciding on the size and design. When they spotted a Grateful Dead collar and leash with the brightly colored bears dancing across it, the choice was made. Mark had a belt with the identical design.

Between the two of them they had barely any money, but they managed to buy a bag of food, two metal bowls, and a couple of cheap toys. There was no need for a dog bed – Mark intended to share his own.

Then they headed straight to the vet.

There were forms to be signed, as well as rabies and micro-chip discs to be handed over. When all the formalities were completed, the nurse briefly disappeared, then returned through a different door with Zeus at the end of a rope leash. He seemed to have recovered from the anesthetic, and his whole rear end wagged when he set eyes on Mark. Mark grinned back and squatted down next to the dog. He stroked his broad head, slipped the dancing bears collar around his neck and attached it to the leash. Then he stood up and smiled proudly at his sister.

"What do you think?" he asked her.

"I love him."

*

Getting him into the truck was no easy matter. Fear made him as stiff as a board, and he refused to get close to the open door. After a few attempts to coax him in, Andrea sat down in the passenger's seat and Mark picked up the stiff-legged dog and placed him gently on her lap. His big brown eyes bulged and his whole body shook all the way to Mark's house. By the time they pulled into the dirt driveway behind the house, Andrea's legs were covered with welts from his rigid claws.

Mark lifted him out of the truck, and as they walked towards the front door, Zeus visibly relaxed. His nose was picking up all sorts of interesting dog smells, and he was curious to meet the dogs behind those smells.

As Mark cautiously opened the rickety front door, the little Pit Bull was met by three eager dog muzzles. The first belonged to Dean, a fluffy Shepherd mix named after Jimmy Dean sausages. Immediately behind him, and reaching from a great height, was a very large black muzzle with droopy jowls. It belonged to a female Great Dane called Memphis. And then, slightly lower than Dean's, and struggling valiantly for position, was the little pointed nose of a small mix named Teddy. The three of them forced the door wide open to greet the newcomer, and after much sniffing and tail-wagging, it was decided: they would be friends.

Hearing the commotion in the living room, Mark's three roommates traipsed in to meet the newest member of their household. It was then that the fun stopped for Zeus. Finding himself face-to-face with three strange men, he backed up quickly, slinking panic-stricken to the safety of Mark's legs. Then, tucking his tail under his shaky haunches, he cowered, miserably anticipating some kind of abuse. In time he would come to trust them all, but for now, they decided to leave him be.

After meeting the roommates, Zeus was taken on a tour of his new home. It was the perfect house for a bunch of dogs. Four young men lived in it, after all, none of them over-concerned with hygiene and tidiness. Dirty dishes were stacked in the kitchen sink, empty bottles were lined up next to the trash can, and the old furniture was dull with dust. They were all seniors at the university, and it was fair to say housework was low on their list of priorities. But they loved their dogs. Mark's housemates had all voiced their concerns about having a Pit Bull in the house, but Mark noticed how quickly their apprehensions were put to rest when they saw how happily Zeus interacted with the other dogs.

*

Andrea looked across the room at her brother. It broke her heart every time she looked at his injured body, but today she could see how happy he was with his new dog. It was funny, but the two of them looked alike. Both of them were short and muscular, and their hair was almost the same color. They looked as if they were meant for each other. Mark had saved the dog's life, but perhaps it could work both ways.

It had been nine months since Andrea had received the terrible phone call from St. Mary's Hospital in Athens. Her brother had been in a serious cycling accident, they said, and hers was one of the numbers they'd been given to call.

She was the first of the family to arrive at the hospital, as their parents had to drive from Atlanta.

"I'm here to see my brother," she said in a barely controlled voice, "I was told I could find him in Emergency."

The receptionist took some time checking papers and lists, then she disappeared behind a set of swinging doors.

When she returned, she smiled kindly at Andrea and told her someone would be coming through to speak to her shortly. Her heart lurched. Why couldn't she see him? She sat down in the waiting area and tried to stay calm.

After a while a nurse appeared, and the receptionist pointed her in Andrea's direction. The nurse came over.

"Are you Mark's sister?" she asked.

"Yes. Is he alright?"

"Well, he has some serious injuries," she said, quite matter-of-fact. "We've just brought him back from x-rays, so we'll know shortly how bad his injuries are. He also has multiple lacerations on his body, and his hands are badly damaged, so they're going to start working on them now to try and stop the bleeding."

"Can I see him?" Andrea asked, her voice shaking.

"I'm afraid not. Do you know if your parents will be arriving soon?"

"I know my dad's on his way. My mom went out without her phone, so we haven't been able to reach her."

The nurse softened a little. "I know this is hard," she said. "I'll let you know as soon as there's any more news, and we'll bring you back to see him as soon as possible."

"Is he conscious?"

"He is now, and he was very happy when we told him you were here."

"Thanks," Andrea managed to say, as the nurse turned away and disappeared through the swinging doors.

She tried to look at a magazine, but it was impossible to concentrate. She stood up and walked over to the window. She couldn't believe people were going on with their mundane activities while this was happening to her brother.

She sat down again, helpless. Time dragged on. From time to time she called her father, but there was little to say.

Eventually, the nurse appeared again through the double doors. She walked briskly across the room and sat down in the chair next to Andrea.

"We've just received the radiologist's report," she said. "Your brother's left femur – that's the thigh bone – is badly broken, and we need to operate as soon as possible. The surgeon is on his way, and they're readying an operating room. I'm going to take you back now to see him, but I must warn you that you may be a little shocked when you first see him. He doesn't look too good right now. He'll be okay, though, once the doctors have patched him up."

Andrea took a deep breath and followed the nurse. She tried to ignore the terrible apprehension that was gripping her insides, but as she walked into the little cubicle, relief washed over her. Mark must have been anticipating her arrival because he was looking towards the door when she entered, and he smiled at the sight of her. Then she saw the blood. There was so much of it, and it was dripping steadily from his hands, which barely resembled hands at all. Every one of his fingers was bleeding heavily, and one of his index fingers looked as if it was barely hanging on by a thread.

She looked away and tried to focus on his eyes. "Hey. How are you?"

"I'm okay," he said, "as long as I don't look at my hands."

"Yeah, I know what you mean," she answered, unsteady. It was hard to talk without crying, and the very fact that he was being so brave made her want to weep.

The nurse bustled back in, carrying a wad of papers. She turned to Andrea.

"These consent forms need to be signed before the surgery can be performed," she explained. "Your brother is unable to sign them – for obvious reasons," she said, nodding in the direction of his hands, "but he says you're over eighteen, and he's happy for you to sign them on his behalf."

Andrea took the forms and began to look them over. As she read through the small print the nasty lump in her throat grew bigger and bigger, and the words began to swim. Eventually she lifted her head, handed the papers back to the nurse and said, "I'm sorry. I can't sign this."

The nurse looked confused. "But why not? Your brother needs this surgery urgently."

"It says here that he could die during the surgery."

"Well yes, that's standard," the nurse explained, "they have to put that in there because there's always a remote chance of death under anesthetic, but it's extremely unlikely. Your brother's young and healthy."

Andrea tried to get control of herself. She knew she was being silly, but she just couldn't sign something that might end her brother's life. "No," she said in a barely audible voice, "I'm sorry. I can't. My dad will be here soon, and he can make that decision. But I can't."

For a moment the nurse looked as if she might try and persuade her, but she seemed to change her mind. She rubbed Andrea's arm and handed her a box of tissues.

"Alright," she said, "I understand." She took the papers and slipped out of the room.

Andrea looked down at her brother.

"I'm sorry," she sniffed, "I just couldn't do it."

"It's okay," he said, with a weak smile. "Dad will do it."

*

Andrea had always been close to her father, but she had never been so happy to see him as she was that day. As soon as he walked through the door, everything seemed better, and she felt she might be able to cope with what came next. She watched as her father bent down over the bed to hold his son. She was glad she had held off signing the papers.

Five
November 2007

Zeus turned out to be an adaptable dog, smoothly adjusting to his new life. And considering his history, how wonderfully strange it must have been for him to be able to wile away his days, sleeping on the furniture with his new companions, and bundling up warmly at night with his new master.

As for Mark, the comfort he derived from having a dog was huge. Though he was surrounded by friends, the constant pain and frustration of his injuries was not something he could easily share with them. Those things he kept to himself.

Living with a disability was extraordinarily hard. Until recently, he'd been an outstanding athlete, accustomed to receiving compliments on his sporting achievements and athletic abilities. But his time as a varsity athlete and state champion wrestler suddenly seemed very long ago, and was painful to recall. For now, his daily physical challenge was putting one foot in front of the other.

He tried hard not to feel sorry for himself, but his self-esteem was battered. He often found himself wondering if he would ever be able to play any sport again, or even walk without a limp. Would he ever be free of this constant, crippling pain? But thoughts like that threatened to take him to a place he could not allow himself to go.

It felt good to have a companion who seemed to share his suffering with him. A dog who loved him unconditionally, never looking at him as if he were not a hundred percent whole. He knew that in the dog's eyes, he was perfect.

He and Zeus walked every day, sometimes with the roommates and their dogs, sometimes just the two of them. Zeus was still not the easiest dog to walk. He didn't pull as hard as he had on their first walks at the shelter, but Mark soon discovered that he was terrified of traffic. He shied constantly as cars whizzed by, sometimes almost wriggling right out of his collar in his attempt to get away from them.

Mark wondered if perhaps he had spent a long time on the streets of Athens, lost and confused, before he'd been picked up by animal control. For a dog who had been tied up all his life in someone's back yard, cars would no doubt have been a frightening discovery for him once he was on the loose. Mark began to take him only on quieter streets with slow-moving traffic, and Zeus soon became a fearless and intrepid explorer, loving his walks. But he did have a disconcerting habit of lunging, without warning, towards any scent that interested him along the way. It was a very annoying habit that was hard to break, meaning no-one but Mark was prepared to walk him.

It was good for both of them. At first, Mark struggled to go just a few blocks, but as time went on he found he was able to keep up, and they began to walk farther and faster. He was having twice-weekly sessions with a physical therapist, which, combined with the walks, was having a noticeable effect on his health. He still limped, but not as badly.

The pain, on the other hand, never let up. Day and night, it was always there. But he had a companion by his side now. A warm and loving soul with whom he could share everything.

Six

Late November 2007

By the time the rest of the family got to meet Zeus, it was Thanksgiving, and he had already been living with Mark for a few weeks. I was in the kitchen at our house in Atlanta when I heard the truck door slam. I dashed out to meet them.

The first thing I noticed was how much Mark's physical state had improved. The last time I'd seen him, he was still walking with a severe limp, his left side pitifully wasted. The accident had shattered his left thigh bone, and the surgeon had inserted a metal rod right through the center of the bone, in the hope it would mend itself and regrow around the rod. Any sort of stress on that leg could have prevented the bone from healing properly, so he hadn't been allowed to put any weight on it at all – or even do physical therapy – for six months after the accident. Since then, he had been slowly learning to walk again.

The second thing I noticed was the sparkle in his eyes. He was excited to introduce his dog to me, and he looked so proud. I crouched down to say hello, but the sudden movement scared the dog, and he lurched away on his leash to hide behind Mark.

"He's still nervous of strangers," Mark explained, "but he'll settle down quickly."

"How will he be with Rambo and Lucy?" I asked, a little worried.

"He'll be fine. He's not scared of other dogs."

I tried to open the kitchen door quietly, but our dogs had already smelled the stranger outside, and they shot through the doorway to meet him.

Rambo was a big, beautiful Doberman Pinscher. He was a sociable character and he generally liked other dogs, but he didn't seem too sure about having a stranger come into his kitchen. The hair on his back rose up and he walked around the intruder stiff-legged, smelling him. Lucy, our fluffy little long-haired Dachshund, yapped loudly, only to scoot under the table when Zeus tried to sniff her.

"Let's take them outside," Mark suggested. "Rambo should be less territorial out there."

And indeed, after a lot of sniffing and strange greeting rituals, Rambo wandered off and lifted his leg on the closest bush. Zeus followed and they took turns lifting their legs around the back yard.

Once the dogs had relaxed with each other, we moved inside and sat down to chat. I was anxious to find out how Mark had been coping with school. I'd been worried about him getting to and from class, and I also wanted to gauge his mood. He'd confided in me that he'd been feeling quite down since his accident, but he'd been adamant he could deal with it on his own.

We had barely started talking when Greg, my youngest son, came wandering into the kitchen. He broke into a grin when he saw his brother, and they hugged – awkwardly, as boys do. They chatted for a bit, then Greg casually turned to me.

"Oh yeah, Mom," he said, "there's a big pile of dog poop in the living room."

"Really?" I asked, horrified, "and I take it you chose not to clean it up?"

"I just saw it right now," he laughed.

I marched through to the living room, and sure enough, there it was, right in the middle of my Persian rug.

"Mark!" I shouted. "Isn't your dog house-trained?"

"Uh, no," he admitted, "not a hundred percent."

I was horrified. I didn't want a dog messing all over my house.

"He's nearly there, Mom," he pleaded, "I had to train him from scratch. I don't think he's ever lived inside a house.

He must have been tied up outside all the time. But he's doing really well. He just makes the occasional mistake."

"Okay," I said, taking pity. "But you've got to clean it up. He's your responsibility."

It wasn't the last mess in the house, and I probably never knew about half of them, but he did make fewer mistakes as time went by.

*

I was trying hard not to become too attached to the dog because I was still planning to find him another home. But he was very engaging, and despite my trying to resist, I was warming to him. Ever since Mark brought him home, I had had a nagging feeling that I'd seen his innocent face somewhere before. There was just something strangely familiar about it. Then one day as I was idly watching the dogs interact with each other in the kitchen, it suddenly struck me.

"Zeus looks just like Winnie-the-Pooh!" I exclaimed.

My husband and children looked at me skeptically, but then I saw them register the same thing. They hauled out all their old Winnie-the-Pooh books from the bookshelf and leafed through them, and sure enough, apart from the ears, there was a strong resemblance. Smiles spread across their faces as they hugged him and laughingly called him "Pooh Bear" and "Winnie".

"If we dressed him in a little cut-off red sweater, you could hardly tell him apart from the Disney Pooh Bear," Andrea laughed.

For a while we nicknamed him Pooh Bear, but it didn't stick. Instead, we started to call him Cubby – because of his resemblance to a little brown bear cub. Sometimes Cubby got shortened to Cub, or Dub, and it soon became Dubby. He answered happily to anything close.

He would sometimes slip into the kitchen while I was cooking, and sit down, neat as a cat with his tail curled tidily around one haunch and his front paws touching. There he would stay, following me with his big brown eyes. He knew how to be a companion.

I also couldn't deny that he had made Mark very happy at such a wretched time in his life.

I had to admit that just a few years ago I'd been against getting a Doberman. The rest of the family had had to persuade me to drive down to McDonough, Georgia, to see the litter. When we'd stopped outside the gate, an intimidating male Doberman had come out and barked at us, keeping us nervously in the car, and strengthening my conviction that a Doberman wasn't a good idea. Once the breeder had escorted us in, though, we'd discovered that the frightening dog was the father of the litter, and far from trying to intimidate us, all he wanted to do was lick our faces as we bent down to look at his puppies.

It was Rambo who had chosen us in the end. At all of eight weeks old, he had tottered purposefully across the yard and looked straight up at us as if to say, "I'm your dog. We can go now."

Rambo was a wild puppy, and an even crazier adolescent, but as he matured I got the impression that he had come to a decision. The decision, it seemed to me, was that his role in life was to take care of me. I could see it in his eyes; in the way he watched me and followed me around. It was a gift, and I felt profoundly grateful.

He grew into a beautiful dog. Tall and strongly built, but with an easy-going temperament. He loved everyone – he seemed to think that all visitors had come expressly to see him – and everyone got the same welcome, whether they were old family friends or the plumber's assistant who had come to fix a leak. He liked other dogs too, and he had friends all over the neighborhood. If someone left the back door open by mistake, he would saunter out and take himself for a walk around the neighborhood, visiting his girlfriends.

After a few days at our house for Thanksgiving, Zeus became very attached to Rambo. It was interesting to watch him follow the bigger dog around. He was about half Rambo's height and he would sometimes walk right between his front and back legs, sliding under his chest. But the most endearing thing was the way he would cuddle up next to Rambo when they lay down. He seemed to want constant contact with the big Doberman, and Rambo seemed quite happy to have him there.

It was Lucy, however, who was in charge. Her little chest cleared the ground by only an inch or so, but she walked with a confident little swagger, her feathery tail held high like a flag. Despite her pint-sized stature, she took no nonsense from either of the bigger males, bossing them around with a cheeky look in her eye. She enjoyed wielding her power. Knowing neither of them would consider stealing her food, she would sit next to her bowl and wait until they had both gobbled their own food down, then slowly enjoy hers while they watched. If they ever bothered her, she would jump up and snap at them, and they would back off, embarrassed. It was funny to see a tiny Dachshund putting a Doberman and a Pit Bull in their place. But there was never any question of insurrection. After chastising them, she would go over and lick their muzzles to show there were no hard feelings, and they would wag their tails and return the kisses.

*

One of the traits most Pit Bulls seem to share is their affinity for games, and Zeus had a real gift for playing. He was strong, and he had the extraordinary ability to leap high into the air, and with all fours off the ground, wiggle his body from side to side before landing nimbly and continuing with the game. Spinning, bucking, jumping and wiggling were all part and parcel of his games. Rambo enjoyed the games, but he couldn't do tricks like Zeus – in fact, he played quite a lot of the games from a lying-down position.

I loved watching them play, but there was something about Zeus that puzzled me: I couldn't remember ever having heard him bark. While Rambo made all sorts of happy growling noises during their games, Zeus was quite silent.

"Mark," I said one day, "I don't think I've ever heard Zeus make a sound. What does his bark sound like?"

"I've no idea," he replied. "I've never heard him bark or whine. The only time I've ever heard him make a sound is when he's asleep. Sometimes, when he's dreaming, he'll make some small yipping noises. If I hadn't heard those, I would have thought he was mute."

"That's very strange," I said. "I've never heard of that before."

"I know. The only thing I can think of is that his previous owners must have punished him every time he barked."

We looked down at him, curled up between Rambo's long legs. His eyes were closed in little straight lines and he looked completely relaxed. Mark had done much more than save his life, I thought; he had given him peace and happiness. I wondered if we would ever hear his voice.

One afternoon, towards the end of the Thanksgiving break, I wandered into the sunroom and sat down to rest my feet for a few minutes. As I did so, I heard the sound of Zeus's nails on the wood floor, and watched as he walked a little hesitantly into the room. He came right up and stopped in front of me. Then he sat down and stared at me with soft brown eyes. His ears were quivering, and his bottom lip, which protruded ever so slightly, added to his sorrowful look. His expression was one of deep worry, as if he knew that his future was in question, and that I had some control over it. I stroked the strong muscles in his cheek, and sighed.

"Okay," I told him, "I know Mark wants to keep you, and I promise I won't do anything to stand in the way of that."

He blinked at me, then lay down heavily, and placed his chunky little head on my foot.

Seven

A Fresh Start

My concerns about Mark's readjustment to life in Athens had, in fact, been justified. After the six-month hiatus in his life, his return had been harrowing on many levels. Though he was happy to get back to living independently of his parents, he was also filled with apprehension about coping on his own, incapacitated as he was. And coping was hard.

His accommodation, luckily, posed no problems. He had kept up his rent payments during his absence, so he'd been able to move right back into his room in the old blue clapboard house he and his friends rented on Oconee Street. There was virtually no lawn left around the house, so the front yard had become a convenient dirt parking lot, which meant he had only a few yards to walk from his car to the front door. And the house itself had no steps at all.

Getting to his classes was not quite so easy. In the past, he had walked to class, but the business school was a good distance away; he knew that wasn't an option now. Driving himself to class was out of the question as parking was impossible anywhere close to the building.

The university provided free transport to students with disabilities. At first, Mark had resisted anything that might classify him as being disabled, and he had explored every other possible option for getting to the school. But finally, he was forced to give in, and he had reluctantly contacted campus transit and established his eligibility. It hurt, though, to accept this small defeat, and he hated the little van that carried him to class.

Resisting the label was a small act of defiance, but it didn't help the fact that he was, undeniably, disabled. In August, the surgeon at last gave him permission to start putting weight on his left leg, but, from the waist down, the muscles on the left side of his body were badly atrophied, and ahead of him still lay the massive task of retraining every one of them.

He constantly replayed in his head the conversation he had had with the surgeon the day after his accident. The surgeon's wording had been careful, but the message was quite clear: it was possible Mark would never walk normally again.

He began physical therapy to start wakening the muscles, and slowly teaching them to respond to his demands. At first, the lack of response was terrifying, and he was beset by the fear that they may never respond at all. But little by little they began to do what he asked of them, and first one crutch, and then a few weeks later, the other, was discarded. It felt good to walk upright again, without the discomfort of the crutches in his armpits, but he still harbored a lingering fear of walking without them and putting trust in his bad leg.

He also discovered, to his distress, that without the crutches, he was just a person with a withered leg and a horrible limp.

People were never openly unkind, but he felt that they looked at him differently – or worse, just glanced at him and looked away, as if really seeing him might spoil their day. There were times, in a crowd of strangers, that he felt almost invisible. And yet, it was hard to believe he could be invisible to others with a throbbing pain in his hip so intense it felt like a visible thing in itself.

Pain is, of course, invisible from the outside, but it is sometimes possible to recognize when someone is trying to escape their own torment.

Downtown Athens, with its charming Victorian-era buildings, is just a few blocks square, featuring a marvelously diverse assortment of restaurants, boutiques and coffee shops, and a remarkable number of bars. It's also directly across the road from the main university campus. During the school year, the nightlife in these few square blocks is legendary, especially for those students who have reached the magical age of twenty-one, and can legally pass through the doors of the many bars and order a drink with impunity.

Mark was delighted to be back in the swing of Athens life. The bars pulsed with energy, and he constantly bumped into friends and acquaintances. When he was seated on a bar stool, no-one was aware of his injuries, and he was able to forget, temporarily, about his problems. But best of all, he found that alcohol numbed the pain.

It wasn't long before he was spending way too much time in the bars. Thursday, Fridays and Saturdays were big nights downtown, and it was always easy to find someone who wanted to go for a couple of drinks. One or two drinks easily turned into a night of binge drinking, and so it went. His drinking was starting to get out of control, and he knew it, but the lure of a pain-free and care-free evening always seemed to triumph over the will to take control.

Just as he was beginning to get a hold on one part of his life, he felt like he was losing control of another. How fortuitous, then, that at this critical juncture in his life, a small Pit Bull should inadvertently cross his path, and, without even trying, have such a profound effect on his decision-making?

*

Even in the early days of their relationship, before he had formed a notion of owning the dog, Mark had started forgoing nights out and going to bed earlier in order to get up in time to visit the pound before classes began. But it soon became much more than that. Outside of Mark's volition, Zeus somehow lodged himself in a part of his mind, and he lingered there night and day. He seemed to fill the space in Mark's heart that had been gaping since the day of the crash.

And when Zeus's warm body literally took up residence in Mark's room, so Mark took real control of his own life. It wasn't a slow, subtle shift, but rather, a singular turn-around in his behavior.

The love and empathy he felt for Zeus translated into a heartfelt sense of responsibility, and the reckless partying lost its appeal as he focused his energy on his dog, instead of himself. For the first time in his life, he was holding himself accountable for someone other than himself.

Having had to be cared for himself for so long, it seemed he now felt the need to bestow the utmost care on this dog who had also suffered so much. He would never really know Zeus's story, but he suspected it was grim, and he was determined to make up for it. The change this relationship brought about in both of them was remarkable. They healed alongside each other, and they healed each other.

Eight

No Trouble at All

By the time Christmas arrived, we knew Zeus was going to be a permanent member of our family. The earnest, round face peering out of the passenger window of Mark's truck had become a familiar sight. The two of them stuck together all the time now – except during class, when Zeus would wait, curled up on Mark's pillow where his scent was strongest.

After finishing his last exam of the semester, Mark loaded his dog and his bag into the truck, and headed home. Zeus still had to be coaxed into the truck, but he endured the hour and a half ride from Athens to Atlanta, dribbling profusely and throwing up from to time. Mark had learned early on to keep a few old towels close at hand.

By the time they pulled into our driveway, Zeus was looking frayed, and eager to have his paws on solid ground. He stepped carefully out of the truck, acknowledged the greetings from Rambo and Lucy, and tottered through the house to the back yard. He always recovered quickly, but cars were a misery to him.

*

We had made a last-minute decision to take the family to Costa Rica for the Christmas break, and Andrea's dear friend Lizzie had agreed to come and stay in the house and take care of all three dogs. Lizzie had known both Rambo and Lucy since they were tiny puppies, and they adored her. She didn't know Zeus very well yet, but she'd met him once or twice and she felt confident she'd be able to take care of him too.

Zeus still chewed things if he was left alone for long periods, so we decided he should be kept in a crate whenever Lizzie was not around. Also, it didn't seem wise to leave a Pit Bull and a Doberman alone together, just in case they had a disagreement.

The Caswells – our friends who lived down the road from us – had a large metal crate which they no longer used for their black Lab, Bentley, and they offered to lend it to us for the week. Bentley wagged her tail amiably as she watched Mark haul it away. She seemed happy to see it go.

The first day went by without a hitch. When Lizzie climbed into bed that night she felt quite comfortable about caring for the three dogs. It seemed like a fun way to make a little pocket money for her next semester.

The next afternoon she decided to go out for a couple of hours. Zeus's crate was upstairs in Mark's bedroom, and Lizzie enticed him up the stairs with a handful of treats. When she got him in the room she tossed the treats into the crate. He dashed in to get them, and she quickly closed and latched the door behind him. He spun around and looked fearfully at the bars around him. Lizzie realized with a pang of guilt that it probably reminded him of his cage at the pound. She felt horrible locking him up behind bars, but she had no choice. She couldn't be at the house every minute of the day.

She turned her back on his accusing eyes and went downstairs. On her way down, she pulled the old mosquito screen across the stairs and clamped it in place. We used this as the barrier to keep Rambo and Lucy from going upstairs when no-one was home. It was just an old window screen, but it was the perfect height, and it had worked well for years.

Lizzie gave the other two dogs each a treat before heading out the door. She felt sorry for Zeus, but she felt comfortable knowing he was contained, and that the males were separated.

*

When she arrived home later that afternoon, she was stunned to find Zeus in the kitchen with the other dogs. He looked as happy as can be, and welcomed her home with a look of complete innocence, as if everything was perfectly normal.

She turned towards the stairs to see if perhaps she had forgotten to put the screen in place, and let out a small gasp. The screen was right where she had left it, but in the center was a big hole, about the size of a Pit Bull's body. He had obviously blasted right through it.

But she was still confused. She knew for sure she had latched the door of his crate.

She pulled the useless barrier aside and started climbing the staircase with three interested followers at her heels. She peered nervously into Mark's room and discovered that the whole top of the crate was lying on the floor next to the crate itself.

Lizzie sat on the bed and looked down at Zeus. "Are you kidding me?" she asked him.

His tail thumped the carpet as he looked at her happily.

She was bewildered. In fact, she never did work out exactly how he managed to do it. She could only assume the crate had never been properly assembled in the first place. How could a dog disassemble his own crate?

She spent hours trying to figure out what to do, but she kept coming back to one glaring fact: Zeus did not want to be separated from Rambo, and he would go to extraordinary lengths to get to him if he was.

*

The next day she called up Betsy Caswell and explained her problem. Betsy could tell that she was on the verge of tears.

"I really love the dogs, and I'd like to take care of them," she explained in a rush, "but I can't just stay at the house all the time, especially over Christmas. And Rambo and Zeus play really rough, and I'm too afraid to leave them alone together in case they get mad with each other."

"No, Liz," Betsy responded in her soothing Southern drawl, "that's not going to work. Just bring Zeus over here."

"Every time I go out?" she asked hopefully.

"No, just bring him to our house and we'll keep him," Betsy said. "There's always someone at home, so he won't ever have to be left alone. He and Bentley get on just fine – in fact it'll be good for her to have a friend to play with."

Lizzie was stunned. She knew the Caswells were kind people, but this was way beyond what she had expected.

"Really?" she said. "You don't mind?"

"Not at all. We'll enjoy having him. Just bring him over with his food and anything else he'll need, and then you can just take care of the other two."

Lizzie felt a huge wave of relief. She didn't waste a moment attaching Zeus to his leash and walking him up to his new temporary home.

*

Neither Lizzie nor Betsy breathed a word to any of us about the dog fiasco until we got back from our trip. Then we sat in stunned silence as Lizzie described Zeus's Houdini-esque antics, and explained that he had moved in with the Caswells.

Mark dashed over to their house, hoping his dog hadn't performed any similar tricks while enjoying their hospitality. He rang the doorbell and peered through the glass. Almost immediately Bentley came ambling towards the door with a teddy in her mouth, and behind her was Zeus, looking quite at home.

Betsy and Charlie Caswell came into the kitchen then, shooing the dogs away so they could open the door. They both wore big smiles as they invited Mark inside, in their usual hospitable fashion.

He thanked them profusely for coming to Lizzie's rescue and taking his naughty dog into their home, but they waved away his thanks. They assured him that the pleasure was all theirs, and they claimed Zeus had been a perfect guest. Of course, Mark would never know if that was true or not, but what he did know was that there are some people whose kindness knows no bounds.

When Zeus got home, he bounced around at the sight of Rambo, and the two of them flew around the house and played crazy games until they flopped down, tongues lolling out the sides of their mouths. Then they snuggled up close, lay their happy heads down and slept.

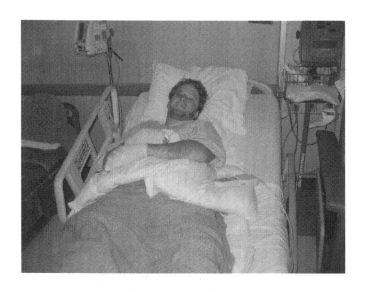

Nine

Undeterred

Rambo was not alone in his growing attachment to Zeus. Even Rory, who sometimes took time to embrace new dogs, had quietly become smitten with the little Pit Bull. It wasn't unusual to hear him chatting to him as one would to a small child, telling him how very much he loved him.

I had noticed that Rory was spending less time on his bike. For years he had been a keen, even passionate, cyclist, but since Mark's accident it seemed that passion had been snuffed out, and that his heart was no longer in it. When he had arrived at the hospital on the day of the accident, he had immediately signed the consent forms to send Mark into surgery, but the shock of seeing his son so badly injured had been profound, and as time went by, he seemed less and less inclined to get on his own bike.

Mark, on the other hand, was determined to prove that this accident was not going to hold him back.

*

When we'd first brought Mark home from the hospital, he'd been confined to a wheelchair, but he had hated being wheeled around, and within a couple of weeks he had managed to find a way to get himself around on crutches. It should have been impossible with a broken elbow and such badly injured hands, but he was determined, and we hadn't tried to stop him.

It was around this time that he hobbled up to me one day and asked me to drive him to the triathlon store. I looked at him in surprise.

"What on earth for?" I asked.

"I want to go and choose a new bike," he told me. "I have a pretty good idea of how much the insurance will pay out for a replacement bike, so I'd like to go and have a look."

Hiding my horror at the idea of him getting back on a bicycle, I agreed to take him. We went through the painful ordeal of getting him into the car, which we then had to repeat in reverse when we got to the other end. I held the door open for him and he crutched his way into the store.

When he got to the middle of the shop, he paused to rest, and it was then that we noticed that all the people in the store had stopped what they were doing and were staring at Mark. No doubt they all guessed he'd been in a cycling accident.

One of the sales assistants stepped forward.

"Can I help you with anything, Sir?" he asked, a little skeptically.

"I'm here to choose my new bike," Mark answered.

There was a moment's hesitation, then one of the other salesmen butted in. "You're what?" he laughed. But there was more than a touch of admiration in his disbelieving laugh.

I looked over at Mark and saw how ridiculous the situation must appear. Here was this person with most of his front teeth broken off, one leg dangling and the other tracked with staples, and two heavily bandaged hands precariously holding him up on his crutches. And he had just announced that he was looking to buy a bicycle! I started laughing too, and pretty soon we were surrounded by customers and sales associates wanting to know what had happened, and if he really planned to ride again.

Yes, he did. And he pretty much knew which bike he wanted. He was just here to look at it and pick the color, so he could dream of being back in the saddle one day. It would be a great incentive for him to get better.

Ten

Spring 2008

By the following spring, Mark was looking remarkably well. It was a little over a year since the accident, but unless you looked closely at his hands, or paid careful attention to his walk, you wouldn't have known what he had gone through.

The surgeon in Athens was extremely happy with his progress. Although Mark's left leg was now half an inch shorter than his right, at least it was straight and strong. The pain was still a big issue, but at this point the overall picture was the best outcome we could have hoped for.

He also, finally, had a full set of teeth. Of all his injuries, the damaged teeth had taken the longest to repair; the force of the impact had damaged not only the teeth themselves, but also the bones in his upper gums. Two of his teeth had required fairly simple crowns, but the third had been so badly broken that it had required an implant and a bone graft as well. It had been a lengthy and taxing process. The oral surgeon had refused to begin the work on his mouth until his gums had healed, and then, after each small surgery, Mark had had to wait three months or more before the next step.

During this whole drawn-out period, he had had temporary teeth that looked passable, but they fell out or broke with frustrating regularity, and often at the most inopportune times. The joy of finally having three new, permanent, teeth was indescribable. His smile was back.

*

Curiously, at the same time Mark was struggling with his dental woes, we discovered that Zeus, too, was having tooth trouble.

We had been taking our dogs to North Fulton Veterinary Hospital for almost twenty years by the time Zeus came into our lives, and shortly after Mark adopted him, we took him for a check-up. The clinic was a small, prefabricated building set back in the woods – simple and unpretentious, but fully equipped – and in Dr. Barger's hands, his patients received the best of care.

Dr. Barger had taken care of all our dogs over the years and we had a lot of respect for him, not only because of his ability as a vet, but also because of his kind and sympathetic approach to his patients and their owners. He and his wife had a large brood of children, and their family seemed to grow larger every year; the first time Zeus met him, they were expecting baby number twelve. Apart from birthing and rearing all the children, his wife also home-schooled every one of them. Quite often, the older children would help out at the animal clinic, and they were always charming and cheerful.

When Mark and I dragged Zeus, petrified and shaking, into the exam room, the vet looked a little surprised, but not overly so.

"Who do we have here?" he asked as he bent down and ran one hand over Zeus's back.

He began his careful examination as we explained how Zeus had come into our lives.

"I know he has Pit Bull in him," Mark said, "but he's so small. Do you think he's a mix?"

"I don't know," the vet said thoughtfully, "he looks very much like a Pit Bull to me. Sometimes they are just small."

When he checked inside Zeus's mouth, he frowned with concern. "Look at these two large molars towards the back of his mouth," he said as he pulled Zeus's lips back. "They're broken. One of them badly so. He must be in some pretty serious pain."

Even a layman could see that the teeth were broken, and one of them was brown and decayed too.

"What do you think we should do?" Mark asked.

"This one will have to be removed," Dr. Barger replied, "but I think I can repair the other one. That way he can hold on to it for a while. I hate removing these big teeth, but there's no choice with this one. These dogs have a pretty high pain tolerance, but even he must be in a lot of pain right now. He'll be a happy dog once this tooth's out. Apart from that, and the fact that he's still underweight," he said as he rubbed Zeus's ears, "I'd say he's in good health. He seems like a sweet dog."

Zeus did seem happier once his tooth was removed. It wasn't the end of his tooth problems, though: over the years he would have to have quite a few broken teeth removed. Not long after the first extraction, one of his little front bottom teeth fell out by itself, giving him quite a comical look. It kept him looking youthful too, like a first-grader waiting for his big teeth to grow in.

Eleven

A Small Bark

It was a few weeks later that Mark called home, full of excitement.

"Mom!" he exclaimed, "I just had to call and tell you. Zeus barked today!"

"He did?" I laughed. "Tell me about it."

"Well, he was playing with the other dogs in the yard, and a bark just kind of popped out by mistake. But Mom, the saddest thing happened then," he added. "The minute he heard his own bark, he stopped playing and stood dead still. Then he looked at me nervously, and I could tell he was expecting to be punished. I patted him instead, and told him what a good boy he was."

"Poor little fellow," I said. "I hate to imagine what his life must have been like before. But tell me – what did his voice sound like?"

"A typical Pit Bull voice," he laughed. "Real gruff and throaty."

I couldn't help smiling at the thought of it. "I can't wait to hear it," I said. "I hope that won't be the one and only."

*

It wasn't the one and only. As it dawned on him that he wasn't going to be punished for making a noise, he tentatively started trying out his voice. At first he would try a small bark and then look quickly at Mark to make sure it was okay. But with a little encouragement he quickly became quite bold, loving the sound of his own bark and delighting in the joy of his new-found freedom. Sometimes he would bark, and then run in a happy circle, his tail wagging and his little square head held high.

Twelve

May 2008

Mark graduated from UGA in May of that year. By then, he was back on a bicycle, and riding regularly. At first, I had tried to object to his riding, but I'd eventually come to see that it was an integral part of his recovery, so I'd decided to hold my tongue.

"Lightning never strikes twice in the same place, Mom," he'd told me lightly. But I knew it couldn't be easy for him to ride again.

As I watched him disappear down the road on his shiny new bike, I shut my mind to the possibilities and forced myself to think of other things. He had plans to move to California at the end of the summer, so I was going to have to stop worrying about him, and let him get on with his life.

I suspected that his desire to move to the other side of the country was also an important step on his road to recovery. He wanted to get away and be completely independent. To cope on his own. But more than that, he wanted to grab hold of life and make the most of it, after having come so close to losing it altogether.

The hard part, for him, would be saying goodbye to his dog. He told himself it would be a short-term separation, and Rory and I had agreed we would care of Zeus until Mark was able to find a place where he could keep a dog. But we knew how expensive Los Angeles was, so we had our doubts about the longer term. In the meantime, though, the plan was for them to spend the summer with us, so it would be an easy transition for Zeus when Mark left.

*

One evening, when Mark and Zeus were cuddled up watching television, I joined them on the couch. Mark was looking a little teary-eyed.

"What are you watching?" I asked.

"Pit Bulls and Parolees," he replied. "I can't watch this show without getting all choked-up."

"I know what you mean," I said. "I can't either."

The show was a reality TV series about a Pit Bull rescue center in California, where they employ ex-prisoners to work with the dogs. Many of the episodes are heartbreaking as they show the actual rescues of Pit Bulls from the most shocking situations, most of them in pitiful condition. The center is full of such dogs. Hundreds of them.

The ultimate aim of the center is to heal and rehabilitate the dogs to the point where they can be adopted, and it is fascinating to see how the dogs respond to the care and training. But I think the most moving part about the show is that both the dogs and their carers are being given a second chance at life. I know that's what resonated with Mark: getting that second chance, and making the most of it. It was something he felt intensely, and it began to steer his decision-making to a very large degree.

Thirteen

Fall 2008

Mark stood by the open door of the airplane, feeling that familiar rush of anticipation as he waited for the signal. His heart beat a little faster as he glanced down at the dun-colored desert that stretched out beneath. Then, when the signal came, he launched himself into the clear California sky.

After struggling for so long with the limitations of his injured body, he had embraced skydiving with an intense passion. It was a sport in which he could participate completely unencumbered by his injuries. There was an element of risk involved in it, too, and that was something that had always attracted him. Moreover, because each jump required such intense concentration, he was able, for the duration of the jump, to completely forget his almost constant pain.

Every Friday, as soon as could, he would leave the confines of his Los Angeles office, jump in his car and head towards the desert. There he would stay, till sundown on Sunday, doing as many jumps each day as he could afford. He bought his own second-hand rig, and learned how to fold his own parachute. In this way he whittled his expenses down to the cost of the jumps alone.

The incomparable combination of pure freedom and adrenalin rush was intoxicating, and no matter how many jumps he did, he could never get enough. Before long he was doing group jumps and formations, and once even jumped from a helicopter.

California suited him well, at least in terms of the lifestyle it offered. He could surf in the morning before work, cycle in the evenings and jump out of airplanes all weekend. From his twelfth-floor apartment the view was panoramic: when the weather was fine, which it generally was, he could see the Hollywood sign clearly from his balcony. On the wall of the living room he hung a large, square color portrait of Zeus. The little dog stared intently from the picture, one ear up and one ear down. The picture dominated the room.

He missed Zeus. He missed the comforting companionship of his dog.

*

Back in Atlanta, Mark's brother Greg ambled out of his bathroom and headed towards his bed. As usual, the side he liked to sleep on was already taken by the chunky figure of a Pit Bull.

"Come on, Cub," he complained, "you know that's my place. You're gonna have to move over."

But moving wasn't part of the Pit Bull's vocabulary. He opened one eye, then shut it quickly in the hope that he'd be left in peace.

Greg shoved both hands under the inert body and shifted it over, then he hopped into the nice warm spot and pulled the covers up.

He watched as Zeus stood up, made a few circles, then curled up again into a tight, egg-shaped ball. Then he slid over and wrapped his arms around him. He liked sharing his bed with a dog, especially this one. He was solid, but soft too, and his compact little body was very, very warm. It was the kind of body that you wanted to hug close to you. Solid, soft and warm, and so very comforting.

Originally, when Mark had first moved out to California, the plan had been for Zeus to sleep with the other two dogs. Rambo and Lucy each had a big cozy mattress in the laundry, and they loved their beds. During the day, Rambo would very often take himself off to his bed for a nap, and, in the evening, he would always disappear into the laundry when he felt it was time to retire for the night. More often than not, Lucy would abandon her bed during the night and snuggle up next to Rambo, leaving her mattress vacant. Considering the fact that Zeus spent most of the day lying right next to, or on top of, Rambo, the assumption was that Zeus would join them on the two big mattresses at night.

But that assumption was wrong. Sweet, amiable Rambo was not prepared to share his mattress with his friend. If Zeus so much as approached Rambo's bed while he was resting on it, he'd be stopped in his tracks by a soft growl, and Zeus, disappointed, would back out of the laundry and lie down forlornly outside the door.

So Zeus got to sleep with Greg.

Now, as Greg lay on the bed, absent-mindedly scratching Zeus's ears, he began to think about Mark, and how much he must be missing his dog. His determination to step out of his comfort zone and go live in California seemed admirable to Greg, and he understood why Mark had gone. But he also knew how much this dog meant to him.

Though the boys were eight years apart, they were good friends. Greg had always looked up to his older brother, and still did, despite the fact he was now several inches taller than him. They were both good athletes, and this alone had made them close. Greg had always admired the way Mark conducted himself on the sports field, and even more so on the wrestling mat, and Mark had encouraged Greg in all his athletic activities. They understood each other well.

When he'd heard the news of Mark's accident, Greg had been devastated. He was determined to go up to Athens so he was there when Mark came round after surgery. If it had been the other way round, he knew his brother would have been there for him.

He remembered the surgeon coming into the little room where they'd waited for hours and hours. The surgeon looked exhausted, but he spent a long time describing Mark's injuries, and explaining how they had done their best to put him back together. Later, when Mark was settled in his own room, the vast assortment of monitors humming and beeping around him, the family had come in to huddle closely around the bed.

Greg's stomach lurched when he got his first look at his brother. Three of his front teeth were completely broken off, with small jagged ends sticking out of his upper gums, and there was a large graze over his right eye. Thankfully, the rest of his face was unhurt. But resting on his chest, where his hands should have been, were two massive white bandages with just his fingertips poking out of the ends. One of his index fingers was unbandaged, and in the small space between the knuckle and the first joint, four metal pins stuck out at odd angles.

Greg's eyes traveled down to Mark's right shin, where an angry laceration about six inches long was being held together by a row of scary-looking metal staples. But the worst injury could not be seen. The damage to his left leg was hidden inside, and the wound in his hip, where the surgeon had inserted the long titanium rod, was covered with a simple white dressing.

They stayed for a long time around the bed, despite how late it was. Huddling together, giving one another strength and reassurance, while monitors beeped in the background, and nurses bustled in and out. Eventually, reluctantly, the family parted, leaving their mother to stay with her wounded son. After dropping Andrea back at her room, Greg and his dad had headed back to Atlanta.

Fourteen

Partners in Crime

Winter 2008

Every afternoon, after having fixed small, medium and large meals in small, medium and large bowls, I would clip three leashes to small, medium and large collars, and leave the house in a cacophony of barks. It wasn't as if I had a choice. The dogs all knew that after meal-time it was "walkie-time", and if I tried to get out of it, they would make my life a misery.

Three pairs of brown eyes would be fixed on my every move, and if I gave the slightest hint of moving towards my closet, where my walking shoes were kept, or the laundry, where the leashes were, pandemonium would break out. They would not have let me walk them separately, or even two at a time, so I had to learn to walk all three of them together.

At first, it was quite a circus. Rambo and Zeus were both very strong and not shy to pull, and on top of this, their legs were such different lengths. The two males would usually be out in front, with Lucy trailing behind, and I would have to walk with one arm stretched forward, and one backward. We soon became a well-known sight in the neighborhood, and strangers would often stop to say how funny it looked to see three such different dogs walking together. Keeping the leashes from getting tangled up was also a challenge, and I was constantly juggling them from hand to hand as they zig-zagged along, chasing after smells on the sidewalk.

One afternoon, having walked with my friend Ellen and her dog Buck, we stopped at the curb outside our house to finish our conversation. As Ellen and I chatted, the dogs wandered around our feet, sniffing aimlessly and growing bored. Eventually we said our goodbyes and turned towards our respective houses. To my surprise, I found that my ankles were completely tangled up in the leashes, and instead of taking a step I fell headfirst onto the grass. I pulled myself up, furiously swearing at the dogs, but before I could untangle the leashes from my legs, I lost my balance again, this time rolling sideways onto the street, where I continued to roll, pulling the three dogs along with me, finally coming to a stop a few yards down the road.

I struggled to my feet, feeling very foolish and more than a little indignant. The dogs, of course, were close by, looking curiously at me, wondering what crazy thing I would do next. Then I looked over at Ellen. She had a funny expression on her face, which at first I interpreted as grave concern. But then, once she'd confirmed I wasn't hurt, she bent over with her hands on her knees, and laughed until the tears ran down her cheeks.

As I pulled myself together, straightening my clothes and brushing the grass out of my hair, I began to see the humor in it, and I sat down on the grass and laughed as the dogs snuffled around, clearly relieved to see me behaving myself.

*

By now, Zeus and Rambo had developed such a strong bond, they were almost inseparable. Whenever Rambo lay down to rest, Zeus would be right next to him. Sometimes he would lie by his side, resting against the bigger dog's chest and belly. Other times he would lie right between his front paws, so that Rambo would have to rest his big head on Zeus's back. More often than not, though, he would plonk his little square bottom right on top of Rambo's chest or shoulders, and sit there happily on top of his friend. Strangely, Rambo didn't seem to mind. After a while he might groan a bit and move, causing Zeus's bottom to slide down to the floor. But then they would curl up close together and sleep peacefully.

Zeus had unquestioningly accepted Rambo as the boss, so there were never any battles for dominance. He was Rambo's sidekick, looking up to him with adoration.

He followed the Doberman wherever he went, doing exactly what his big friend did, unless it entailed something a little scary. He was always a lot braver when he and Rambo were together, but he was still very cautious, and whereas Rambo considered every stranger a potential friend, Zeus was still deeply fearful of them.

He was, however, happy to enable his friend in his daring pursuits. The gate to our driveway had a spring that caused it to shut automatically, but Zeus had somehow worked out that if it was not properly latched, he could open it by delicately poking a paw between the vertical bars, then pulling back on the horizontal bar at the bottom. In this way, he would open the gate, let Rambo out for an adventure in the neighborhood, and let the gate swing closed, staying safely behind it himself. It was some time before one of us actually saw him in action and we were able to work out how it was that Rambo kept getting out.

By then, we'd gone through quite a few frantic neighborhood searches, one time even going as far as making signs for a lost Doberman and hanging them on lampposts. A full five hours after we'd noticed his absence, someone called the house in response to one of the signs. She had seen a Doberman wandering around in the sub-division behind ours. He must have found his way through a couple of different yards and navigated around a large retention pond to get there.

I thanked the lady profusely, jumped in my car and drove over, barely heeding the stop signs and speed limit on the way. Then I slowed down and painstakingly patrolled each street, calling his name as I went. I spotted a boy I knew from the wrestling team, and he leapt on his bike and took off searching in a different direction. I waved down a couple in a passing car and asked if they had seen my dog. Yes, they confirmed. They had indeed seen Rambo, but he was a scary-looking dog and not for a moment had they considered calling him over to check his tag. On the contrary, they had steered well clear of him.

I had almost lost hope and was calling frantically when I turned the corner and rolled into a short cul-de-sac. I looked one way, then the other, and then I saw him. He was in deep shadow so he was hard to see, but he had heard my voice and was standing dead-still, looking towards me with his ears up. I stopped the car, opened the door and ran towards him. We met halfway, and I laughed until I was in danger of crying. He was a mess. His lovely shiny coat was dirty and scratched up. It was clear he'd had a marvelous adventure.

After that, we rigged a dog-proof latch on the gate, and Zeus was no longer able to aid his friend in his efforts to escape.

Despite being such a confident dog, Rambo also had a very needy side. He thrived on love and attention, and in the same way that small children find comfort in a special blanket or pillow, he found comfort in our dirty socks. As soon as a member of the family removed a sock from their foot, he would carefully pick it up with his front teeth and carry it around for hours. Very seldom would he chew it. He would simply carry it around from place to place, and keep it with him. He also had a fondness for my kitchen towels. I always kept one or two hanging on the handle of the oven door, and I would sometimes catch him tugging one off and carrying it away.

Once, when he knew I'd caught him at it, he ran off with it in his mouth, and dashed up the front staircase with Zeus tagging along behind him. I heard Rambo pounding along the upstairs passage, and Zeus pattering after. Then there was a loud crack, and a couple of wooden spindles fell down the back stairs, followed by my kitchen towel. I ran up to see what had happened, and found Rambo wandering around, looking a little dazed and confused, and the remains of two broken spindles on the railing at the top of the stairs. Zeus was looking equally confused, no doubt wondering why the game had come to such an abrupt halt. As for me, my only conclusion was that the kitchen towel had flapped up over

Rambo's eyes as he was galloping down the passage, causing him to run blindly into the railing.

Fifteen

Zeus About Town

Not long after Lizzie's unfortunate experience taking care of our dogs, my friend Meg started up her own pet-sitting business. Rambo and Lucy were her very first clients, and although she was soon the most sought-after pet-sitter in the area, we believed our dogs maintained a special place in her heart.

Meg loved her job from the start, joking about how she had the best clients in the world. Every one of them, she told us, would meet her at the door, ecstatic, tails wagging and mouths wide open in candid expressions of delight. Who could dream up nicer clients than that? And in return, she would do whatever it took to keep them safe and happy. She seemed to understand each of her charges, pandering to their likes and dislikes, their funny quirks, fears and habits.

The first time we went out of town after Zeus had moved in with us, we decided he would have to stay in the kennel. Lizzie's experience of him breaking out of his crate to get to Rambo was still fresh in our minds — and he tended to chew our rugs if he was left alone for too long. We didn't think it was fair to leave Meg in charge of a rug-chewing Houdini, so Zeus was booked into the kennel close by and Meg took care of the other two as usual.

But Meg hated the idea of his being in the kennels on his own.

"I'll visit him," she told me. "I'm not that busy at the moment, so I can pop in and see him every day."

"Oh Meg, that's not necessary," I said. "He'll have playtime with some of the other dogs each day, and the staff like him. He'll be fine."

"I know, but I'm afraid he'll think he's been sent back to the pound, and I couldn't bear that," she explained.

She insisted I write a letter giving her permission to visit him, and even to take him out during his stay. I knew her intentions were good, but I also knew she didn't really have the time. I assumed she'd probably forget about him soon enough. I wrote the letter anyway.

When I picked Zeus up from the kennels a few weeks later, the receptionist took off her glasses and looked at me.

"Zeus had a visitor almost every day. A lady who took him out for long walks and sometimes even on outings in her car!" She was clearly very impressed. "First time I've ever seen that."

And that explains why he was seen on several occasions during our absence, riding in the front seat of a baby-blue Thunderbird with the top down, his ears flapping gaily in the breeze, as he cruised around the streets of East Cobb.

*

Of course, it didn't take long after that for Meg to try to persuade us that she could take care of all three dogs.

"But Meg," I argued, "Zeus will destroy the rugs, and then I don't know what Rory will do. We may be looking for a new home for the poor dog!"

"You and I will make sure he doesn't chew the rugs," she told me patiently.

Her plan was to move all the furniture and rugs out of the kitchen and sunroom area, and then to barricade all the doors. We left a couple of old cushions and cheap scatter rugs in the room, and then Rory and I left town with our fingers crossed.

"It worked!" Meg told me happily on our return. "Look at the little guy! He's so much better off at home with his buddies."

I nodded as we lugged the furniture back into place, puzzling all the while over how this little abandoned Pit Bull had managed to get us to completely reorganize our lives around him.

But Meg was clearly delighted. "I wish you could have seen me walking all three dogs," she laughed. "One day I decided to try this special leash that goes around your waist," – and she picked up an odd-looking blue leash from the table and clipped it around her middle. Then she went on to explain how she had attached Zeus to the special leash so she could hold Rambo's leash in one hand and Lucy's in the other.

It had apparently worked quite well. But as she'd turned the corner and started to head up the hill with the three dogs, she'd seen a friend coming down the other way in his car. John had never been much of a dog lover, and was, in fact, rather afraid of big dogs. He'd slowed down to talk to her – looking at the scenario in an amused, horrified sort of way.

"Am I going crazy?" he'd asked her from the safety of his car, "or have you really tethered yourself to a Pit Bull?"

Sixteen

February 2009

After a year and a half in California, Mark decided to return to Atlanta and work for his dad. Not only had he missed Zeus, the other thing missing from his life was that elusive, perfect job that he'd been so certain he would find out West.

After his close shave with death, he had made an unequivocal decision to never waste a moment of his life doing anything he didn't love, and had vowed to find work that was exciting and different. His degree was in finance, but a financial institution was the last place he wanted to work. He found a flashy-sounding job with an agency in Los Angeles that placed screenwriters with movie companies. But the job had turned out to be nothing like he'd imagined, and was utterly unsatisfying. Going to work every day had become a miserable trial, and not having been able to find a job he loved was a source of deep disappointment.

Physically, he had made good progress since the accident, but the hip pain – which had seemed to be abating – was strangely back with a vengeance. For me, the relief of having him close by again was enormous.

When he first returned from LA, Mark stayed at home, with us and Zeus, while he looked for a place of his own. Each night Zeus could choose whether to sleep with Mark or Greg. If Andrea was home she would always take him to sleep with her.

He was a good bedmate because he slept so soundly. But he hadn't always been quite such a perfect sleeping partner. When Mark had first brought him home from the pound he had wanted to stay as close to Mark's face as possible, cuddling right up on the pillow and breathing into his neck and shoulder. Slowly Mark had encouraged him to move down, little by little, and as his confidence grew he was content to sleep closer to the foot of the bed.

When none of the kids were home, he slept in our bedroom. Rory and I didn't like sleeping with a dog on our bed, so I would make a cozy little nest for him on the floor next to my side of the bed. He would curl up in a tight ball and wait for me to cover him with a soft fleece blanket, then he would close his eyes and sleep like an angel, barely stirring. In the morning we would allow him to jump up on our bed and snuggle between us for a while, but he would never jump up until he was invited.

He was a ridiculously sweet dog. He had such an air of vulnerability. I found that every little bit of him tugged at my heartstrings, from the bulgy little muscles beneath his ears, to the neat rows of whiskers on his jowls. From the quirky kink halfway down his tail, to the splayed fingers of his front paws.

It was impossible to look at him curled up next to us, and not feel a huge welling of affection.

*

Now that Mark was back, living at home, we were coming round to the possibility that he might be living with a disability, and likely with constant pain, for the rest of his life. I was having a hard time accepting this realization.

In the immediate aftermath of the accident, I had had to be very strong, mentally and emotionally. In fact, apart from the initial panic when I heard the news of the accident, I had only once broken down and allowed myself to cry.

It was two days after the accident, and Mark and I had just woken up from a quick nap. The nursing staff had moved a surprisingly comfortable couch-bed into his ward for me to sleep on, and I was spending pretty much every minute by his side. As I was readjusting his pillows, I noticed his right elbow was very puffy and bruised. The nurses were constantly popping in and out, so the next time one came in to check his vital signs, I asked her to take a look.

"I'll talk to the doctor and order an x-ray," she said. "It doesn't look good to me."

They wasted no time in calling radiology, and it wasn't long before two women in green uniforms arrived with a wheelchair in tow. I was shocked to see the wheelchair.

"You're not going to move him, are you?" I asked. He had an IV in his left arm, which was feeding all sorts of fluids into his bloodstream, and he was connected to numerous machines.

"Yes Ma'am," they answered, "that's the only way we can get a picture of his elbow."

I watched, uneasy, as they heaved him off his bed. Excruciating pain was etched onto his face, despite the morphine drip which had until now been keeping it under control.

Once they had wedged Mark into the wheelchair, they whisked him out through the door, the IV trundling along on its own set of wheels.

I stayed in his room, trying not to imagine what they were doing to him in the x-ray department. I hoped they had some strong men down there who could move him more gently.

They didn't. When they finally wheeled him back into his room, his face was a pasty white, and sweat was running down his cheeks. They maneuvered him into his bed and he lay back, eyes shut and chest heaving. I bustled around, trying to make him comfortable, but I could tell that the pain was out of control.

When his nurse came in, she discovered that his IV needle had been dislodged, and the morphine was no longer dripping into his bloodstream, but was instead uselessly draining into the tissue of his arm, causing it to swell alarmingly.

"I'm sorry, Mark," she said, and I could see she was genuinely upset. "I'm going to have to take this out and get it back where it should be."

But it was easier said than done. His arm was so swollen from the fluids that his blood vessels had almost disappeared from sight.

She tried a couple of times, but gave up. There was no question of inserting it into his right arm because that was already hugely swollen from what would, in fact, turn out to be a fractured elbow.

"If we can't get the IV back in we'll have to change to oral pain meds," the nurse told me. "They're not nearly as effective, but they're better than nothing. I'm going to get a nurse from ICU to try first, though," she said as she dashed out the door. "They're really good at finding blood vessels."

When the ICU nurse came in, I left the room and sat outside the door. I had begun to feel like I might be sick, or pass clean out if I continued to watch. I heard her talking to Mark, and I could tell she was trying and trying to get the needle in, but eventually she gave up too. I heard him thanking her for her efforts.

"I'm going to get one of the nurses from the lab," she told me as she left. "This is what they do all day. They'll be able to get it in."

When the lab nurse arrived, I left the room again, and took my seat outside the door. From the conversation she was having with Mark, it was evident she was also trying very hard, and I did my best not to imagine her stabbing his poor arm over and over again. Eventually, though, I gathered that she, too, had given up, because I heard him thanking her for trying, and telling her not to worry.

It was this small thing that ultimately caused me to lose the tenuous grip I had had on my own composure. That quiet and polite "thank you" from behind the curtain.

I put my head in my hands then, and wept.

*

Later that same afternoon, I left the front entrance of the hospital and took a walk around the block a couple of times. It felt good to breathe in the fresh air and to watch people going about their usual activities. I felt decidedly more relaxed as I climbed back up the stairs to the second floor.

As I left the stairwell and turned towards Mark's section, I noticed two uniformed men coming out of his room. They were young men with pleasant faces, and I heard them politely thanking the nurse on duty as they passed by the nurses station.

"Who were those two men who just left your room?" I asked Mark as I walked in.

"Oh Mom, I'm sorry you missed them," he said. "They both tended to me at the scene of the crash. Such nice guys. They came to check on me."

His voice was lively; I could tell he was very touched by their visit.

"Firemen or medics?" I asked.

He looked a little baffled. "I don't know," he said, and it occurred to me that his mind was probably fuzzy from all the painkillers they had given him after his horrendous morning.

"Well, whoever it was," I said brightly, "it was very nice of them to come and see how you were doing. Did they tell you anything interesting?"

He nodded and turned to look out the window. "They told me that the guy who hit me is a retired firefighter," he said, frowning.

"Do they know him?" I asked.

"No, I don't think so. I guess he must have told them."

He was quiet for a while, and I guessed he was trying to imagine the scene.

"They said he didn't see me until I actually hit the front of his truck. He was turning into the entrance to the post office, and he just turned right into me. They said he was really upset about it."

"I'm sure he was," I said. "What else could they tell you?"

"They said I was unconscious when they got there, but that I opened my eyes as they were lifting me onto the gurney."

"It's funny," he continued, "I can remember the ride in the ambulance, but I can't remember hitting the truck."

"I'm sure that's a good thing," I said.

"I guess so," he replied, still staring fixedly out the window.

"Can you believe it?" he said at last. "An ex-fireman! He spends his whole life saving people, then he nearly kills me."

I shook my head at the irony of it.

"Maybe he'll come and see me," he said hopefully. "I'd like to meet him."

Seventeen

April 2010

Two and a half years on, Mark's second hip surgery was not as urgent and traumatic as the first, but neither was it the "piece of cake" the surgeon implied it would be.

It was an exact reversal of the original surgery, as the pin was removed from his hip, and the long rod extracted from his femur. What no-one explained beforehand was that the entire muscle in the side of his hip would have to be sliced through in order to reach the head of the femur and pull the rod out.

But the surgery had become a necessity. The pain had grown intolerable, and x-rays had shown that the rod had moved and was causing friction inside the joint. This wasn't a big surprise. His surgeon in Athens had warned that if he became very active, this was likely to happen. Every jump out of an airplane requires a landing, and every landing, no matter how skilled, involves some jarring in the hip.

And so, Mark found himself back on crutches, this time waiting for the tissue to reknit so he could once again train his muscles to walk.

Pain and frustration are lonely things to bear, and Zeus understood this in the instinctive way that dogs do. As Mark hobbled around the house, or laboriously made his way up and down the stairs, Zeus was always a step or two behind him. Though he never got in the way of the crutches, he always managed to stay within touching distance. It was as if he knew all about sadness, and understood that his unobtrusive presence would help.

When Mark started physical therapy, Zeus sat close by, watching earnestly as Mark slogged his way through the painful regimen of exercises. From time to time, as he caught his breath between sets, he would call Zeus over and scratch his solid little chest, or bend down and rest his forehead on the soft, bulgy muscles on the top of the Pit Bull's head. Then he would grit his teeth and start on the next set.

*

A few months after moving back home, Mark bought a house of his own in Candler Park, closer to downtown Atlanta. It was a half-hour drive from our house, and we all held our breath, nervously waiting to see if he would take Zeus to live with him.

"He is your dog, and you have every right to take him with you," we told him, desperately hoping he wouldn't.

But it didn't take him long to decide. "No," he answered with certainty. "I'd like nothing better than to take him with me, but he belongs here now. Look how happy he is. I couldn't make him start all over again in a new house, and I can't separate him and Rambo."

So Zeus stayed, and we all breathed a sigh of relief.

Eighteen

A Place by the Sea

The island of Grand Bahama is a relatively unknown sliver of heaven off the east coast of Florida. Lined with pristine white beaches, it lies shimmering in turquoise water so shallow and clear that the contours of the seabed are clearly visible as you fly overhead. It was here, nestled in a hidden tropical garden by the sea, that we found the home of our dreams.

Rory and I had, for many years, longed for a home by the ocean, and it was around the time that Mark moved back to Atlanta that we found, quite by accident, this perfect place. The house was airy and spacious, had lots of history and charm, and sat on a large, leafy property next to a sandy white beach. As we walked around, we could picture ourselves there in the years to come, surrounded by our children and grandchildren.

It was not hard to tell that the previous owners were dog-lovers. There were five or six elderly dogs wandering around, watching us warily. One had only three legs, and they were all of indeterminate breed. It was then that we heard, for the first time, the term "potcake". Potcakes are the mixed-breed dogs that live all over the Bahamas, the term coming from the thick, congealed cake that remains in the bottom of a pot of peas 'n rice, and which the Bahamians commonly feed to their dogs.

We also learned that the previous owners of the house were the founders of the Humane Society of Grand Bahama, and that, at one time, they had had as many as seventeen dogs living on the property. We couldn't wait to bring our own dogs down. We knew it would be paradise for them.

But for years we didn't bring them. The thought of putting them in crates in the hold of a big commercial airliner was something we could never face, especially knowing how terrified Zeus was of being caged up and separated from Rambo. Eventually, a couple of years later, when we had a small plane of our own, it was a piece of cake to bring the dogs with us, but in the meantime they stayed home with Meg when we went over to Grand Bahama.

Looking back, I so wish that we had taken the chance, though. I would have done anything to see all three of them together on the beach.

Nineteen

A Moment in the Limelight

When Greg graduated from high school, he and four of his close friends decided to have a combined graduation party.

and we offered to have it at our house in Atlanta, around the pool. The moms decorated the cabana in all the colors of the colleges the boys were heading to, and there were big bunches of balloons to represent each of the schools.

As it turned out, the weather was cool and gray, not at all suitable for a pool party, and towards the end of the afternoon most of the remaining guests drifted indoors to the kitchen, where they stood around, chatting.

Rambo loved large gatherings, and had been mingling happily with the guests all afternoon. Lucy had quietly ignored most of the proceedings, while Zeus, who hated crowds of any sort, had been hiding upstairs since the arrival of the first guest. But as the crowd thinned, he quietly ventured downstairs and watched from the sidelines. He wanted to join the fun, but couldn't quite pluck up the courage.

Then, a red balloon caught his attention. It had come loose from its bunch, and some of the boys were idly batting it around the kitchen. Zeus watched silently for a while, then quite suddenly his desire for the balloon must have eclipsed his fear of the crowd, because he dashed into the group, jumped up, and bopped the balloon up into the air with his nose. The reaction was instantaneous. Conversation stopped, and everyone moved to form a circle around him.

His timing and precision were impressive as, time and again, he jumped up on his hind legs and bopped the balloon into the air, then waited for it to float back down. Each time it strayed, a hand would bat it back into the circle for him, and he would lift himself up and bop it again. He was the center of attention, surrounded by smiling, laughing faces, and he was loving it!

I looked across the room at Meg, whose face was wreathed in smiles. We couldn't believe our eyes. In fact, most of the people in the room knew how shy Zeus was, and they all watched his performance with delighted surprise.

But, predictably, the game didn't end happily for the little fellow. In his excitement, he must have pierced the balloon with one of his teeth, because it popped with a mighty bang right in front of his surprised face, and his marvelous toy was suddenly just a sad scrap of red rubber.

For a moment he was paralyzed with fear, then he fled from the kitchen and ran up the stairs to his safe hiding place. It was a pitiful sight and we all felt deflated to see his wonderful game end that way. But oh, how he had enjoyed his moment in the limelight!

Twenty

July 2011

In the heat of the Atlanta summer that year, Zeus developed a strange, persistent cough. At first I didn't pay much attention, because he had always been quite prone to throwing up, and would often make coughing noises prior to getting sick. This time, though, the cough continued all day, and I realized it was something different. He was also listless, and not as keen on his food. I called the vet's office and made an appointment for first thing the next morning.

Dr. Barger listened carefully to Zeus's heart and lungs, checked his temperature and looked at his throat.

"It's a respiratory infection," he concluded as he gently lowered Zeus to the floor. "We'll get him on some antibiotics and you should see a difference within a few days."

"Is it infectious?" I asked as I was leaving. "Zeus and Rambo are always licking each other's mouths, so should I expect Rambo to get it too?"

"It's possible," he replied. "Just bring him in if he starts to show symptoms."

After a day or two Zeus's coughing began to subside and he perked up. His appetite came back, and by the end of the week he was back to normal.

A few days later, just as I had expected, Rambo began to cough. It was late on Wednesday morning when I called the vet's, and I knew they closed on Wednesday afternoons. They had no more appointments that morning, but I wasn't worried; I knew what was wrong. I made an appointment for the next day, and in the meantime, I started Rambo on Zeus's antibiotic.

As the afternoon wore on, Rambo's cough became worse, and he began to look very sick. His little short nub of a tail was uncharacteristically still, and he had it clamped down tight. His head hung low as he paced restlessly around the kitchen, his whole body slumped and sad. I wiped the foamy spittle from his lips, then I sat on the floor with his head on my lap and stroked his big bony head. But nothing seemed to soothe him.

By the time Rory got home from work, it was evident that Rambo was in distress, and we decided to take him to the emergency vet in Roswell.

The journey perked him up, and he rode along happily, looking out the window. As soon as we pulled up outside the emergency clinic he could smell other dogs, and eagerly pulled on his leash to get inside. We looked at each other, thinking maybe we didn't need to bring him in at all. But we signed in and sat down in the waiting area.

Rambo was one of those rare dogs who actually enjoyed going to the vet. He considered everyone a friend, and the people at the clinic were no exception. He greeted everyone with a wag of his little tail and a lick, if he could reach them. There were no other dogs in the waiting room, but he sniffed every inch of the floor with interest.

When we were called into the examination room he showed no hesitation, pulling on his leash and sniffing the new room with equal enthusiasm.

"He seems so much better," I apologized to the nurse. "Perhaps we overreacted a bit by bringing him in, but he seemed really distressed earlier."

When the vet came in he was amused by the eager greeting he got from Rambo, and by his complete lack of fear. "This is one relaxed dog," he joked.

We explained what was wrong, and how we assumed that he had picked up the cough from his friend. The vet nodded his head. "He probably just needs something a little stronger."

He knelt down on the floor, placing the stethoscope on Rambo's big chest, and listened for a long time to the sounds inside.

When he eventually straightened up, his demeanor had changed, and we could see there was something that he really didn't want to say.

"This is not a respiratory infection," he said quietly. "Rambo has a heart condition known as cardiomyopathy. It's very common in Dobermans. In fact, it's so common amongst his breed that it's often called 'Doberman cardiomyopathy'. His heart has stopped functioning correctly, and his lungs have started to fill up with fluid, which is causing the cough."

My first instinct was not to believe him. "But our other dog was coughing just like this," I said accusingly, "and he's fine now."

"Pure coincidence," he said, not unkindly. "I'm sure your other dog did have a respiratory infection. But what Rambo has is something completely different."

He looked at us regretfully. "I need to take him back to do an electrocardiogram. You can wait here. I'll bring him back as soon as we're done." Then he picked up the leash and led Rambo through the door.

We sat quietly in the examination room, telling ourselves that the vet must be wrong. Neither of us knew much about cardiomyopathy, but we knew it couldn't be good.

It wasn't long before he returned. He told us that the ECG had confirmed what he already knew. He showed us the printout and we stared unseeingly at the rows of squiggles.

"I'm going to keep him overnight," he said. "We'll get him started immediately on medication to try and regulate his heartbeat, and we'll get him on oxygen too."

He was a kind man, and I could see from his hesitation that what he had to say next was very hard for him. "I'm going to bring Rambo back here for a few minutes," he said, "and I'll leave you in peace to say your goodbyes."

It took us both a moment to understand his meaning. The shock must have shown on our faces, because he said, "I'm not saying he won't make it through the night. I'm just saying that it's possible that he won't."

"But we love him so much! He's such a good dog!" I blurted out stupidly, as if that might change the diagnosis.

"I know," he said. "We'll do everything we can."

*

We drove home in a daze, determined to believe Rambo would be okay in the morning. We weren't ready for this. He was only eight years old – in the prime of his life. And we loved him too much. We felt terrible for leaving him there. Did he wonder why we were deserting him when he needed us the most? We wondered how much dogs understood of human emotions. Had he understood what our tears had meant as we hugged him and kissed him, and inhaled the smell of his coat?

*

The phone trilled at six o'clock the next morning. Rory grabbed the receiver and we were both immediately wide awake, fearing the worst. It was the animal clinic. Rambo had made it through the night and was doing okay, but could we please come and get him as soon as possible and transfer him to the Veterinary Specialists in Sandy Springs? Yes, we could. We smiled with relief.

I pulled on some clothes and ran down to Greg's room to tell him the good news. Then we jumped in the car, buoyed by the fact we would be seeing him again.

The night duty vet at the Specialists clinic was still there when we brought Rambo in. He examined our big boy and confirmed the diagnosis. Once again, he was led away from us into a back room where they would continue with the drip and the oxygen. They encouraged us to call for updates any time and told us we could visit him in the afternoon.

*

When we got home, Zeus and Lucy were right inside the door, but we realized right away that it was not us they were anxiously waiting for. Their greeting was polite, but cursory, and they pushed past us to look out the door. We watched as their ears and tails drooped with disappointment. Then they turned around gloomily and followed us inside.

We both pulled out our computers, frantic to get onto the internet to see what we could find out about Rambo's illness. There was no shortage of information, but no matter how much we searched, there was no good news. The best hope we could find was that he might survive on medication for a few months.

That afternoon, Greg and I went to visit him. A nurse showed us into a little visiting room and then went away to get him. When he walked into the little room, we knelt down, eagerly anticipating his excitement at seeing us, but he looked so sick, he didn't even have the strength to wag his short tail. He was wearing a thick black vest that resembled the bullet-proof vests soldiers wear. It covered most of his body, so we were only able to stroke his big old head, which hung down, utterly sad and worn out. Every now and then he would try and lie down, but the pressure on his chest was too much and he would begin to cough, then stand up immediately. It looked as if his legs could barely hold him up, but lying down wasn't an option. We realized that he was utterly exhausted.

I felt a kind of desperation welling up inside me. The only way I could think of to ease his distress was to make him lean against me and to try and take the weight off his legs by supporting him with my arms. Greg and I took turns doing that, but it was very awkward, and we weren't sure if it was giving him any relief at all.

This time, when the nurse led him away, I knew there was no hope.

At six o'clock the next morning, the phone rang again. This time my heart dropped and landed in the hollow pit of my stomach. I watched my husband in the half-light as he listened, frowning into the phone. Then he took a deep breath and said, "We'll be there as soon as we can."

I watched him as he slowly put the phone down and turned to me.

"Rambo survived the night, but he hasn't responded to the treatment," he said steadily. "The vet feels that he's reached the point where he's no longer treatable."

There was a moment when, knowing he was still alive, hope tried to push its way into my mind and fool me into thinking he still might make it. But it was fleeting. I knew there was only one thing we could do for him.

"We have to put him to sleep," I said.

"We don't know that for sure," Rory replied, hope obviously getting to him, too. But I had seen him the day before, and I did know.

The thought of what we were going to have to do was almost inconceivable, but I also knew it was the last kindness that we could bestow on our beautiful, loyal dog.

We drove to the clinic in dismal silence.

The vet met us in a little private room, and I told him we had made our decision. Rory didn't speak much, and I knew he wasn't convinced we were doing the right thing. The last time he had seen Rambo was the previous morning when he'd still had life in him and was eagerly sniffing the new clinic.

"Do you think there's any hope at all?" we asked the vet.

"No," he answered gently. "You're doing the right thing."

Then he went on to explain, with infinite kindness, what the procedure would be, and exactly what we should expect.

"Rambo is no longer able to walk," he said, "and I don't want to move him, so I'm going to take you through to the back." We nodded and followed him, numb.

When we came to his cubicle we found him lying on his side with the drip still feeding the medicine into his front leg, and an oxygen tube in his nose. He'd reached the point where he couldn't even lift his head off the floor, but his eyes followed us, and we knew he knew we were there. He looked so very tired. We could see that every breath was an effort.

The cubicle was tiny, but we managed to wedge ourselves in and kneel down next to him. We stroked and stroked the beautiful black head that was so dear to us, and we whispered into his ear, telling him how very much we loved him. I pushed my face into the soft rolls of skin on his neck and breathed deeply, inhaling for the last time the distinctive, comforting smell of him.

After a while, the vet came quietly back into the cubicle. Rory got up and stood behind me, giving him space to kneel down. As he attached the syringe to the drip line and prepared to push the blessed poison into his bloodstream, I slid my hand under Rambo's dear, sweet head and brought my face right up close to his. It seemed very important that I should say something he would understand, so I scratched him softly behind his ear, just the way he liked it, and as I did so, I told him over and over what a very good dog he was.

And he was.

Twenty-One

Summer 2011

It took many months for Zeus to get over the loss of Rambo. It was extraordinary and heart-breaking to see him waiting and listening for his friend to come home. Day after day he waited at the door, and then eventually we saw him give up hope. His bouncy, happy demeanor seemed to fall away and he became quiet and listless.

We knew it was not just that he was missing his friend, but that he had also lost direction. His compass was gone. For nearly three years he had followed Rambo around, taking his lead in almost everything. Suddenly, he was completely lost.

Lucy had also loved Rambo, and she too waited expectantly by the door. But she had never been as dependent on him as Zeus had, and she coped far better.

We decided Zeus should start sleeping in the laundry room with Lucy, and he was content enough to take over Rambo's old mattress. He and Lucy had always gotten along fine, but they had never been overly interested in one another. Now, with Rambo gone, they became much more attached, cuddling up together and finding comfort in each other's company. But even so, our bouncy little Pit Bull had become a lost soul, and we weren't sure how to help him.

*

The turning point finally came months later, when Rory and I went away for the weekend and Mark offered to take care of the dogs for us. By now Mark had a few friends living in his house and two of them had dogs, including Dean, the fluffy Shepherd mix, who was already a friend of Zeus's from Athens days. There was Reptar, too, who was young and eager to play, and who made friends quickly. The weekend away, playing with Dean and Reptar, seemed to snap Zeus out of his misery, and when we brought him home we could see his old, happy personality starting to peep through again.

The other thing that helped him was that he found a new friend. Not a replacement for Rambo, but a dear little friend who could play with him every day and make him feel like life was fun again.

One of a litter of six abandoned mongrel puppies, Bosley was as lucky to be alive as Zeus himself. He and his siblings had been dumped in a cardboard box and left by the side of a busy highway in Alabama. Through remarkable good luck, they were spotted and saved by a young college student on her way back from a football game. By even greater luck, by nightfall Bosley had found himself living a life of luxury in the adoring arms of Betsy and Charlie Caswell, alongside their sweet-natured Lab, Bentley.

One can only imagine what went through his little head as he snuggled into his warm and cozy crate that night with a full tummy and a first notion of human love.

With his bright face and bouncy step, Bos cavorted around the Caswells' house with unrestrained joy, as if he knew how lucky he was. Like his new friend, Zeus, he had an uneven pair of ears, and when he pricked them up, one would fall comically forward, almost covering one eye. He was smaller than Zeus, but tough, and he was happy to play the Pit Bull-style wrestling games Zeus loved. When the two of them had worn themselves out, they would collapse on their sides with their tongues hanging out, and take a nap side by side.

We watched as Zeus's confidence and interest in life grew back.

Twenty-Two

Fall 2011

Zeus had a powerfully strong neck, and sometimes, if he was particularly happy to see you, he would throw his head from side to side as he wiggle-trotted across the kitchen towards you. It was this cheery sight with which Andrea was greeted one day after having not been home for some time.

At the sound of her voice, Lucy came scampering into the kitchen too, and both the dogs broke into a jubilant dance.

Andrea knelt down to accept their gestures of love, all the while trying to protect her face and body from unintended injury. Eventually they half-calmed down, and Lucy was happy to trot in circles, occasionally lifting her nose in the air and letting out a little howl of joy, while Zeus plumped his little backside onto Andrea's lap.

"Hey, you little nugget," Andrea said as she rubbed Zeus's firm flanks, "your body's shaped just like a cylinder! How'd you get so porky?"

She looked accusingly at me. "Mom, you've let the little guy get fat!"

"Yes," I admitted, "Dr. Barger weighed him last week and he has gained a few pounds. I've started him on a lighter food so I'm sure he'll lose weight soon. It's hard not to give him treats, though. Just look at that face!"

Andrea kissed the top of his chunky head and he turned to look at her. He had never understood the concept of personal space, and he stuck his nose right in her face. She wrapped her arms around his body and held him close. "I love you, Mister," she murmured in his ear.

"And you too, Missy," she said as Lucy stood up on her hind legs and rested her paws on Andrea's arm.

"It sounds like Mark has found himself a dog," I told her when I was able to get her attention.

"I know he's been looking," she said. "He wants to rescue a Pit Bull again, and he's been searching the websites of all the rescue organizations."

"He called just before you walked in the door," I said. "He says he's found the perfect dog. He told me to check my emails. He's sent a photo of her."

I opened my iPad, pulled up my emails, and there she was. I could tell from first glance that she was, indeed, perfect. She had a marvelously unique face, and spread across it was the widest smile I had ever seen. Her muzzle was white, but she had large gray patches over both eyes, and her eyes themselves were a pale hazel. Her ears had been cruelly trimmed into sharp points, but her face shone with happiness. Her name was Grace.

Mark had come across her on Petfinders.com. He made contact with her foster mother, and received the following reply:

> Gracie is very sweet and social. She does well with other dogs, and watches cats, but has never gone after one. She loves to play fetch with a ball, and loves to get sticks and chew on them, or play tug of war.
>
> Gracie was left at a kill shelter after a rescue took her puppies. The animal control officer was impressed with her good nature, and she asked us to take her so she wouldn't be put to sleep. She is fully house-trained and loves to crash on a pillow near you. If you want to sit and watch TV, she is good with that, and if you want to run, or go to a dog park, she is also good with that. She is very sweet and well mannered.

The email was signed Donna and Gracie.

As it turns out, Grace had already been adopted once, but the couple had separated, and sent her back. Fortunately, her foster mother was a wonderfully kind woman, with a houseful of similarly abandoned Pit Bulls whom she took under her wing until good homes could be found for them. She had welcomed Grace back, and continued the search.

Grace was not pure Pit Bull. The bullet-like shape of her head suggested that she was part Bull Terrier. Her legs and underbelly were white, and the end of her tail looked as if it had been dipped into a can of white paint, but the rest of her was a sleek iron gray. Not everyone would have described her as beautiful, but she certainly turned heads. We thought she was gorgeous.

Though she was built like a tank, she had a remarkably easy-going personality. She was calm, and afraid of nothing. When Mark brought her home, she trotted into our house with a huge grin on her clown-face and won us all over. Zeus loved her from the moment he set eyes on her. Even Lucy liked her immediately. Dean and Reptar liked her too, and she settled into her new life with ease.

For a while, Mark kept regular contact with Grace's old foster mom. He knew she cared about Grace, and he wanted to reassure her that she was happy and loved. He sent her photos of Grace on the beach, on the plane, celebrating Christmas in the Bahamas.

By now we were in the habit of taking Zeus and Lucy to the Bahamas every time we went. They had become so comfortable with the plane ride that they ran up the airplane stairs on their own and sat down in happy anticipation of where they were headed. Zeus liked to sit right behind the cockpit, watching the pilot's every move on takeoff and landing. It was hard to imagine that this confident frequent flyer of ours had so recently been a miserable, drooling wreck in a car.

On our next trip, Grace calmly followed Zeus onto the plane, found a space next to him, and lay down. She kept her eye on the pilot too.

*

The dogs loved the beach more than anything, especially when there was no-one else around and we could take off their leashes and let them run free.

Lucy was an elderly dog by now, but she seemed to shed years as she dashed along the beach like a puppy, skirting the waves to keep her low-slung belly dry.

For Zeus, it seemed like the burden of anxiety would fall away as he stepped onto the sand. We had expected him to be afraid of the waves, but he'd surprised us right from the beginning by embracing the beach fearlessly. He would bravely explore the waves and the scrubby vegetation, but after each foray into the unknown he would trot back to our sides for a little reassurance. We would reach down and rub the soft, rounded muscles on the top of his head and he would look up, giving us a wide, tongue-lolling grin before dashing off for another quick adventure.

Grace loved the beach too, but for her, the greatest thing was the coconuts. Our yard was full of coconut palms, and there were always plenty of coconuts lying around beneath the trees. She would spend hours ripping the fibrous outer layer off with her strong jaws, after which it was a snap for us to crack them open with a machete.

Grace showed us that Zeus's loving nature was not unusual in Pit Bulls. Just like Zeus, she craved physical contact and would sit on, or lean against, humans or other dogs whenever she could. She was a solid, muscular dog, but she saw no reason why she shouldn't climb up on someone's lap, place her head gently on their chest, and gaze lovingly into their eyes.

*

That year, for Christmas dinner, I roasted a whole beef tenderloin. It was a lovely day and we had decided to eat outside. When we were ready to eat, I carved us each a slice and we carried our plates out to the table which Andrea had decorated beautifully in reds and greens.

Mark and Greg cleaned their plates quickly and went back to the kitchen for seconds. They disappeared inside, then poked their heads out the door again.

"Where did you leave the rest of the meat, Mom?" they asked.

"Right on the kitchen counter," I replied, nonplussed.

"We didn't see it there," they replied, "but we'll have another look."

Sure enough, the other half of the roast had completely disappeared. Not a sliver remained on the carving board.

There were three obvious suspects. Lucy was acquitted immediately – she was much too short – so Mark knelt down and sniffed the muzzles of the two Pit Bulls. Zeus passed the test, but Grace's mouth reeked of beef, and the smears of meat juice on her white chin were a dead give-away.

She had gobbled up at least two pounds of premium roast beef and cheated Mark and Greg out of their second helpings, but the culprit looked deeply satisfied, and not the least bit sorry.

*

A few months later, when an elegant black Doberman stepped into our kitchen, it almost took our breath away. At first sight, this new member of Mark's family looked so much like Rambo it almost hurt. He was strongly built, like Rambo, but his nose was longer and more slender, and his gait was looser. He was goofy too, in a most endearing way, and where Rambo had been jauntily confident, Bentley (no relation to the Caswell's Lab) was bashful and sensitive. I felt a deep pang of affection for him as he walked hesitantly up to us, head dipped, asking shyly for a little attention.

Bentley was two years old when Mark adopted him. His first owners had been unable to care for him, and when

Mark had spotted him on the Doberman rescue society's website, he had known immediately that he would take him. How could he not? And anyway, Grace needed a brother!

Twenty-Three

A Different Breed

The first time I found the trash can lying on its side I thought little of it. It was a tall, white plastic trash can which we kept under the computer desk and used mainly for waste paper, and I assumed someone had accidentally knocked it over and not noticed.

The second time I found it tipped over, I was a little puzzled. None of the trash had been removed, and the plastic liner lay perfectly intact. But there it was, lying on its side again.

I picked it up and placed it back under the desk.

It wasn't until the third time that I began to suspect something strange was going on. I was the only one who used the desktop computer and I wasn't in the habit of kicking trash cans over. I was intrigued. I began to make a point of checking on the trash can with regularity, and I noticed it would often be lying on its side after I had been out of the house for more than a couple of hours.

By this time, Zeus had been living with us in Atlanta for about four years. He had settled down beautifully and hadn't chewed anything of value for a long time. I had reached the point where I trusted him enough to leave him the freedom of the house when I went out. He loved lying in the sun during the day, so I often left him sleeping upstairs in a sunny spot.

And so, a pattern emerged: If I left Zeus in the house and stayed out for much more than an hour, the trash can would be lying on its side when I returned. Always facing the same direction, and with the trash still inside, untouched.

I now knew who the culprit was – that much was clear. But the motive? The timing? I was even more curious than before.

I called Meg to tell her about it. She was as amused and intrigued as I was. Why was it always the same trash can?

Did he give it a gentle nudge with his nose, or a belligerent shove with his shoulder? At what point during my absence did he decide to go and tip it over? We longed to know.

The next time we were out of town I received a text message from Meg.

"All is well," it said. She'd sent a photograph of the trash can, lying on its side, facing north, as usual.

*

A few months passed, and one day it occurred to me that the trash can had not been tampered with for some time. I kept a vague eye on it, but it remained upright and untouched. Months went by, and then we left town again for a few days, leaving Meg in charge of the dogs as usual.

As soon as we got back from our trip I called her to let her know we were home.

"Did you see the picture I sent you?" she asked.

"No," I replied, "but I did have trouble receiving texts while I was gone."

"Well," she said, "a certain Pit Bull is back to his tipping tricks. But take a look at the photo. He's changed things up a little."

I looked at my phone. This time the photo popped right up.

"That's funny," I said, "the trash can is lying the wrong way."

"Exactly," Meg laughed. "That's how it's been every day."

I took a closer look. In the foreground was the trash can, facing east-west, and in the background was Zeus, lying on the carpet and looking vaguely embarrassed. Or was it proud?

"By the way," Meg continued, serious, "I had a kind of epiphany the other day. I think I worked out why Zeus tips over the trash can."

"Really?" I said. "Go on."

"Well, it suddenly came to me that he's not a Pit Bull at all. He's another breed, closely related, called a Tip Bull."

I could tell she was on a roll now, delighted with her idea.

"Tip Bulls," she explained, "are smaller than Pit Bulls, and they were bred not to fight, but to tip things over. It explains so many things about our Zeus: not only his small size and lack of aggression, but also the left eye that droops from time to time. It's very useful for eyeing out, from an obtuse angle, the things he has to tip. You can tell, can't you, that I've been doing quite a bit of research into the topic?"

"Yes," I laughed, "a Tip Bull. That explains everything."

Twenty-Four
July 2013

On a wintry afternoon in July of 2013, Rory and I caught the train at the station near my brother's home in Johannesburg, and traveled to O.R. Tambo International Airport in the fading light.

After checking in for our flight to Atlanta, we battled the snaking lines in security and immigration, then made our way out of the clamor and into the relative calm of the departure lounge.

We were spending a lot of time in South Africa back then, as my dad, aged 89, had just suffered a devastating fall. He had rallied, though, and defying all odds, had been moved from hospital to rehab clinic, and would soon be back in his own home. This knowledge had made the goodbyes a little easier.

Now, as we sat down with a glass of wine, waiting for our flight to be called, we decided to make our usual pre-flight calls to our kids.

Rory dialed Mark's number first. He picked up immediately, and although I couldn't catch the words, I could hear an unmistakable overtone of agitation and anger as his voice rose and fell. Rory spoke to him at length, then he quietly hung up. My stomach clenched as I waited for him to turn to me.

"He's okay," he began grimly, "at least, he's going to be alright. He was hit by a car again, and he's not in great shape."

As I hurled questions at him, and he tried to give calm answers, I was able to piece together a sketchy story.

Mark had been cycling in a quiet neighborhood when he was hit from behind. The driver, a middle-aged woman, had been talking on her cell phone. She had passed way too close, and her side mirror had clipped his body with tremendous force, throwing him clean off his bike. She had stopped and expressed immediate remorse – but then, when the police arrived, she proceeded to claim that Mark had swerved right into her car, and there had been nothing she could do to avoid him. Luckily, there had been witnesses who contradicted her, and confirmed that Mark had been well on his side of the road when the accident had occurred.

The driver's attitude was a disappointing and bitter contrast with the genuine remorse that the driver in the first accident had apparently shown after hitting him. Mark had, in fact, never managed to meet the driver of the truck and talk to him, and this was a strong and continuing regret.

But I was still numbly trying to establish the basics of what had happened this time. "Where is he?" I asked.

"He's home. He was taken by ambulance to a hospital in Fulton County. They kept him overnight, then released him this morning."

"That means the accident was yesterday!" I cried. "Why did no-one tell us?"

"He wouldn't allow Andrea and Greg to call us. I guess he wasn't going to tell us until we got home," Rory sighed. "He sounded awful, though. I knew something was wrong."

I put my head in my hands and took a deep, deep breath. Mark had friends to help him, and a girlfriend too, yet I knew in my heart that he needed me, and I wasn't there for him.

But there was no possible way to expedite our homecoming. We had a seventeen-hour flight ahead.

*

When we finally got to him the next day, we found him bitterly angry and depressed. His belief that lightning would never strike twice in the same place had been proven wrong. He seemed shattered by this fact, and profoundly upset by the unfairness of it all.

It had been six and a half long years since the last accident, and he had finally reached a point where he could get out of bed most mornings, feeling healthy and relatively pain-free. This second accident was a massive and overwhelming setback.

When the ambulance had arrived and carried him away with sirens blaring, he had felt as if he were reliving a nightmare. At least this time there was no blood, and no loss of consciousness, but he knew that his bad leg was damaged again, and his whole left side was a blur of pain.

X-rays had revealed a fractured shoulder and torn rotator cuff, as well as three cracked ribs. There were no breaks in the left leg, just contusions and strained ligaments.

Nothing could be done for any of his injuries. Just time and rest. All he could do now was begin the long process of waiting while his body slowly healed itself.

Which, in time, it did.

Twenty-Five

A Super-Hero

"Where's his cape?" Meg asked, her eyes all crinkled up with amusement.

She was sitting in our kitchen, my iPad open in front of her, looking at some photos of our recent trip to the Bahamas.

I looked over her shoulder to see what she was referring to. The photo was one that Rory had taken in his favorite bone-fishing spot. It was low tide and the translucent water was just a few inches deep, leaving the mangroves high and dry. In the foreground, Zeus was trotting toward the camera with a confident swagger, his tail all the way over to one side in an animated wag. Gone was the worried expression he often wore in anticipation of some or other calamity, and in its place was a look of utter self-assurance and joie de vivre.

"Can you see how brave he's feeling in this picture?" Meg asked.

She bent down and rubbed Zeus behind the ears. "You old knucklehead," she said affectionately, "you felt like a super-hero, didn't you? All you needed was a cape flying out behind you."

He thumped his tail and gazed at her admiringly.

She was right. When he was at the beach he was a different dog. He seemed to be able to shake off all the bad memories from his miserable youth and just be happy. Even strangers were not that scary at the beach.

He would run chest-deep into the water, jumping over the waves and digging in the sand. Stray coconuts and bunches of seaweed that floated by would be attacked and vigorously shaken before being thrown aside. Then he might lift his muzzle in the air and bark hoarsely into the wind, for the sheer pleasure of it.

If Lucy was with him he would sometimes herd her, like a sheepdog. Whether he was trying to keep her from drowning, or was just being a pest, we were never quite sure – but he seemed to do it whenever she trotted into the waves.

We knew that strangers on the beach would be afraid of him, so we always took his leash with us and we would attach it to his collar as soon as anyone came near. It was amusing to see how many people rushed to pick up their babies and dogs and give us a wide berth when they saw Zeus coming. We didn't blame them. They didn't know him.

On the other hand, there was a surprising number of people who recognized his sweet nature and stopped to compliment us on his handsome looks. We accepted every kind word with gratitude.

One morning, though, as I was walking near the hotel a little way down the beach, I saw two middle-aged women in bathing suits coming towards me. Zeus was right behind my heel so I reached down to attach his leash, but I had left it slightly late. The women were grabbing onto each other dramatically, and one of them started shouting in a high-pitched voice: "We think your dog should be chained up!"

I started to explain that he was a gentle soul, but I could see from their self-righteous expressions that I was wasting my time. I patted his sturdy little back and turned away, glad that he didn't understand their ugly words.

Feeling unfairly picked on, and not a little hurt for Zeus's sake, I continued an argument with the women inside my head, coming up with some clever one-liners to prove how sweet my dog was.

*

It reminded me of another, quite recent, incident. I was taking Zeus and Lucy for a quick afternoon walk around our Atlanta neighborhood, when a woman I had never seen before came walking towards us with a little male Shih Tzu on a leash. He seemed interested in meeting my dogs, so I gave the owner my usual explanation: "Yes, he is a Pit Bull, but he's friendly and likes other dogs," etc. She told me her dog was friendly too, so we let them greet each other. Both dogs were wagging their tails in a relaxed way and seemed to be getting along nicely, when suddenly, out of the blue, the Shih Tzu wriggled out of his collar and began a vicious attack on Zeus.

Completely taken by surprise, Zeus tucked his tail underneath him and dashed around behind me. He hunkered down and watched, appalled, over his shoulder, as the fluffy white hellion nipped at his exposed rump. He stayed like that, stoically bearing the onslaught, while the dog's owner stood, frozen, holding the dangling leash. She seemed to be expecting retaliation from Zeus, but when none came, she hesitantly pulled her dog off Zeus's poor hunched-up rear-end, and slipped its collar over its neck, all the while assuring me of her dog's gentle nature.

Finally free of his attacker, Zeus straightened up, shot me a meaningful look, then shrugged off the whole nasty incident with a brave shake and continued on his walk. On the way home he stopped to greet June Bug, the terrier on Clarendon Drive; Daisy the Greyhound at the top of the hill; and Daisy the Samoyed at the bottom of the hill. He wasn't going to let one mean dog spoil a good walk.

Twenty-Six

Fall 2014

Mark's second accident, as horribly unfair as it was, turned out to be a blessing. It was exactly the catalyst that he had needed. The quiet time spent on his own forced him to take a long, hard look at where his life was headed, and he decided he didn't like the look of it. Not at all.

Ever since the first accident, his working life had lacked direction, though it wasn't due to bad luck or aimlessness. The decision he had made to never waste a minute on something for which he had no passion had proved to be impracticable, and that perfect job, elusive. A chimera. With great enthusiasm he had leapt into a few exciting-sounding ventures, but they had all been too good to be true. Now he had finally come to the conclusion that the thing that would make him happiest was a solid job with a steady income.

And so, as his body began to heal, he set his heart and mind on a new goal: a master's in accountancy. This would mean going back to school, and he began immediately to study for the GMAT.

For the first time since his accident all those years ago, he was focused, and had a clear vision of what he wanted to do with his life. He once more had the inner energy that had driven him so strongly during his high school years, and a bright light shone in his blue eyes.

He still lives in Atlanta, and has three dogs now. It was shortly after his second accident that he rescued another Pit Bull to save her from being euthanized. She has almost identical markings to Grace, and when asked if he would save her he just couldn't say no. Her name is Olive, and she is the most energetic, enthusiastic dog I have ever met. She loves every minute of every day with a huge passion, and she has a big, loving personality – exactly what we have come to expect of a Pit Bull.

*

Lucy is fourteen now. She still enjoys her daily walks and maintains her position as alpha dog in our household, but her lovely brown eyes are milky and she is almost completely blind. Her hearing is not what it used to be, either, but we suspect she chooses what she does or doesn't want to hear: She never fails to hear "treat", "walkie" or "dinner time", but appears not to hear words like "off" or "outside". Her sense of smell, however, is still perfect. She finds us wherever we are by following our scent, and we can always hear her coming because her tags drag along the floor as she follows her nose on her short little legs.

Zeus's age will always be a mystery – we never knew how old he was when Mark found him. He's a little like Peter

Pan, in that he doesn't seem to grow any older. He still likes nothing better than to play, and although he doesn't jump quite as high, or spin quite as fast, he still wrestles with his friends whenever he has the chance. If he plays too hard he will often develop a limp, but apart from that, and a few white whiskers, these are the only signs he is growing older.

He and Rory have become dead keen gardeners in recent years. He takes an enormous interest in all Rory's gardening activities, particularly if they involve digging a hole, in which case he'll dig his own hole right next to Rory's. If it begins to rain while they're out in the yard, he'll wait miserably while the raindrops fall on him, but he won't go inside until his gardening buddy does.

He is so certain of his place in the world now, and confident in our love for him. His fear of strange men has never really gone away, but he has become an astute judge of character and he decides quite quickly whether or not to put his trust in a new acquaintance.

From time to time, he will form an intense attachment to someone he meets. My yoga teacher, Shailaja, who comes to our house every Monday morning to give me a lesson, is one of the chosen ones. When he hears her car pull up outside, he dashes to the kitchen door, where he whimpers with anticipation until I open it.

As she removes her shoes and lays her bag on a chair, he follows her, barely able to contain his excitement, his tail wagging wildly from side to side. We cannot begin our practice until she has devoted a few minutes to him. She rubs his chest and strokes his head and ears, telling him how much she's missed him since last week. Eventually he calms down. But then, when she sits cross-legged on the floor, he turns around, backs up and lowers his bottom into her lap. And there he stays, his fat little bottom nestled in the gap formed by her crossed legs. A look of pure happiness on his face. Eventually he grows bored with the yoga and moves off to where he can nap comfortably while still keeping us within earshot.

His adoration for Shailaja has never surprised me. She is kind and gentle, and he picked her as his friend the moment she first walked in.

Later, when she leaves, he stands for a moment and looks sadly at the door. But then he turns, the frown of disappointment leaving his brow as he spots me standing there, and he trots happily to my side, which is where he remains as long as I am in the house.

These days, he goes by the nickname Dumpling. I don't remember exactly how he came to be called that, but with his curvy little body and sweet gentle nature, it suits him well.

Recently my brother spent a week with us. He was standing nearby when I called the dogs inside, and I heard him chuckling as he greeted them with a good pat.

"What's so funny?" I asked him.

"I never thought I'd meet a Pit Bull called Dumpling," he laughed.

*

Andrea and Greg have both moved far away; she to Washington, D.C., and he to Boulder, Colorado. I know they miss their family, but I suspect they miss the dogs more. Both their phones are filled with photographs of Zeus doing this or that – and their friends, who've never even met the little Pit Bull, know all about him.

Who would have thought that a frightened, lost Pit Bull on death row would bring so much love and happiness into our lives, and perhaps, in his own quiet way, be an ambassador for his breed?

Epilogue

It is one of those perfect Bahamian days. The sun is shining brilliantly in a flawless blue sky and a tender breeze moves this way and that, taking the sting out of the sun's heat.

On the beach the waves whisper softly up the white sand, hesitate, then slide quietly back into the ocean, leaving just a trace of bubbles behind.

The beach stretches as far as the eye can see in both directions. It is almost deserted. A few little shorebirds scurry along on their skinny legs, searching the sand for food, and the occasional white crab dashes sidelong into a hole.

Farther along the beach, a young man is standing ankle-deep in the waves. He carries a tangle of leashes in one hand, and in the other, a coconut. Behind him is a fluffy little sausage dog, her nose pointing up at his back, and her ears blowing gently in the breeze. She barks excitedly as he wades deeper into the water.

Nearby, in the shallow waves, the light-brown, compact figure of a Pit Bull can be seen jumping over the surf, then alternately biting the foam and frantically digging in the sand beneath the waves. From time to time he stops his frenzied activity to look up and confirm everything is safe.

Then he turns back to the water and resumes his game with wild abandon.

The young man throws the coconut far up the beach and three young dogs streak across the sand towards it. The Doberman has more natural speed, but the gray Pit Bulls are more determined, and they reach it first. They trot back up the beach, and when the coconut has been dropped at the young man's feet, they fix him with eager stares, mouths smiling widely and tails held high with anticipation.

The brown Pit Bull joins them. He has found a long stick and is carrying it proudly between his strong jaws. His step is jaunty. The younger dogs grab onto the stick and the four of them wrestle with it for a while until the older dog grows tired and leaves it to the others.

The young man moves a little way up the sand, away from the water. He turns and whistles softly. All five dogs run across the sand and sit at his feet as he attaches their leashes one by one to their collars. He rubs his hand gently over their heads and ears as he speaks to each of them.

Then he straightens up and walks across the beach with barely the hint of a limp.

81092296R00080

Made in the USA
Columbia, SC
15 November 2017